Romancing the Globe

The Call of the Wild on Generation X

*Dan
Harrison
with
Gordon
Aeschliman*

INTERVARSITY PRESS
DOWNERS GROVE, ILLINOIS 60515

InterVarsity Press® is the book-publishing division of InterVarsity Christian Fellowship®, a student movement active on campus at hundreds of universities, colleges and schools of nursing in the United States of America, and a member movement of the International Fellowship of Evangelical Students. For information about local and regional activities, write Public Relations Dept., InterVarsity Christian Fellowship, 6400 Schroeder Rd., P.O. Box 7895, Madison, WI 53707-7895.

All Scripture quotations, unless otherwise indicated, are taken from the HOLY BIBLE, NEW INTERNATIONAL VERSION®. NIV®. Copyright ©1973, 1978, 1984 by International Bible Society. Used by permission of Zondervan Publishing House. All rights reserved.

Cover photograph: Ron Lowery/Tony Stone Images

ISBN 0-8308-1323-3

Printed in the United States of America ∞

Library of Congress Cataloging-in-Publication Data

Harrison, Dan, 1941-
    Romancing the globe: the call of the wild on generation X/Dan
Harrison, with Gordon Aeschliman.
       p.   cm.
    ISBN 0-8308-1323-3
    1. Youth in church work. 2. Youth in missionary work. 3. Youth—
Religious life. 4. Evangelicalism. 5. Vocation. I. Aeschliman,
Gordon D., 1957-   . II. Title.
BV4447.H335 1993
253'.084'2—dc20   93-41898
                                                CIP

15   14   13   12   11   10   9   8   7   6   5   4   3   2   1
04   03   02   01   00   99   98   97   96   95   94   93

1
The Call of the Wild

Every morning at 5:30 Sandra rolls from her hammock, slips on her Red Wing boots and walks a straight line to the small ring of stones still hot from the previous night's fire. She bends to her knees, blows on the embers. The red glow ignites the twigs, sending a flash of yellow across the backs of her hands. She remains prone while she recites Psalm 121 silently:

I lift up my eyes to the hills—
    where does my help come from?
My help comes from the LORD,
    the Maker of heaven and earth.
He will not let your foot slip—
    he who watches over you will not slumber;
indeed, he who watches over Israel
    will neither slumber nor sleep.
The LORD watches over you—

the LORD is your shade at your right hand;
the sun will not harm you by day,
   nor the moon by night.
The LORD will keep you from all harm—
   he will watch over your life;
the LORD will watch over your coming and going
   both now and forevermore.
Amen.
Day ninety-seven.

The Rain Forest: Sandra's Story

Sandra's morning prayer is sealed with "Belizian Joe," a brew made from her private stash of Seattle's Starbuck espresso beans ground between stones and boiled in water drawn from the north fork of Caves Branch River. As with the other ninety-six days, Sandra settles against "her" mahogany tree for a quiet time and personal journaling. Three years with the Navigators taught her the value of time alone with God at the beginning of each day, and her teammates' nocturnal pattern leaves her with a full hour of solitude before they wake up. Today the team will return to the United States, and in eleven days Sandra will start her senior year of studies in environmental engineering at the University of Washington.

Her final journal entry is titled "A Prayer from Hummingbird Junction." In it she asks God for the privilege of joining nature's choir, to "sing the praises of the King." She ends her entry with a string of Wendell Berry quotes. Sandra has been a part of an academic summer program in the Belizian rain forest and, in her words, it has been an "immensely wonderful" experience.

"I have prayed more times than I can remember," she writes, "that God would give me a place to serve. I've been asking for a place to work in nature, and this summer was everything I was looking for. Something about this place reached out and snagged my imagination.

"Nature is God's. Remember the story of Job, when he was bitter about his suffering? God finally reached Job by asking him to look at the extravagance of creation, to put himself in the care of the one who put that together.

I still remember the day I was having my quiet time and God showed me that caring for the environment was a way to keep God's fingerprints visible to the world. Think about it, I work in the Creator's royal garden."

Once her degree program is complete, Sandra plans to return to Belize as a two-year intern. "After that, it's anywhere for God. I pray that I can be a creation activist for the rest of my life. I'd love to do it somewhere in South America."

It's not surprising that Sandra's life is taking its present course. As far back as she can remember, her family has been active in environmental issues. Not that there was any particular "Christian" angle to it. In fact, neither of her parents follows Christ. But she always assumed she would be doing something for the earth. "I became a Christian during my senior year in high school but it wasn't until my sophomore year at UW that I realized how God had used my parents to prepare me for my future."

Youth and the City: Ian's Story

Ian's morning routine for the past three months has been nothing so romantic as Sandra's. "I sleep with two pillows. One under my head, the other over my ears. It's never quiet. This is a twenty-four-hour city. If it's not the clang and clash of the garbage collectors, it's a siren or a fight."

Ian grew up on a farm near Des Moines, Iowa. The summer after his senior year in high school, he joined other varsity basketball players for a summer of sports outreach in the Philippines. He became hooked on the idea of serving God through his skill and went abroad each of the next three summers. "I didn't start out as a missionary or anything that grand. I liked the idea of traveling to play the courts. But I have to tell you, when you see the world as it really is, it makes you think. It makes you wonder about your life."

Ian's design on the future was, first, professional basketball and lots of money; second, taking over his parents' farm. "Don't get me wrong. I'm not saying I shouldn't do any of that. But something much bigger got to me. How do you just ignore what you've seen? It's as though a snapshot of my first summer in the slums hangs in front of my eyes and says 'don't forget.' I can't walk away from that."

It turns out that Ian has a natural gift with youth. His energy and sense of humor quickly win him a place in the hearts of kids. His summers abroad taught him this. Whereas earlier he would have described his skills as being good on the court and the farm, now he sees that he is also "good with kids." And it goes deeper than just finding a new skill. "Have you ever seen a cow with hoof fleas? It drives them nuts. It's all they can think about. They jump, buck and twist as though something has possessed them. I got possessed a few summers ago, and I thank God for it."

Ian graduated from college with a physical education degree and immediately joined the staff of an inner-city ministry in Chicago. He plans to stay there "as long as God keeps me here." The summer schedule has included a lot of sports, a few field trips, two discipleship camps and some special tutoring for youth who were not doing so well in school. His favorite part was building friendships with youth at risk. "Some of these kids have no one to look up to. It seems that all their authority figures are telling them what's wrong with them. I suppose I'm like a big brother to them—the kind they need but don't have."

Ian is already looking forward to further training. He has had very little formal training in the Scriptures and didn't get a whole lot out of the youth programs at church. "I was your basic terror in basketball shoes. I really can't remember a thing from youth group except the things we got into trouble for. This fall I'll have a chance to get some extra Bible training while our neighborhood kids are in school. I would like to take my kids through the Bible and give them a chance to grow up with a better understanding of God than I had. But they've pretty much already heard everything I know!"

Ian has also joined a local church and is taking advantage of all the discipleship classes. "A year ago I started having personal devotions. It's not that I didn't know about them. It's just that my life wasn't big enough for them. Now I need them."

Long-term plans for Ian include the Philippines. That's the place where God first reached him with a view of the world that is much larger than his own little world, and he feels a special attachment to that country. "You could say that the Philippines gave me a gift—a gift of vision. I owe it something, and I sure hope I'll be able to live there in the future. Who knows, maybe I'll be able to take a bunch of these inner-city youth with me. Wouldn't that be great?"

For now Ian is glad to know he is where God wants him, glad to know he can live a life that really makes a difference in the world. And even though he shuts the world out of his ears at night with a second pillow, he isn't shutting the world out of his heart. "The world has changed me. It got inside my heart and I'll never be the same."

Islam in London: Karen and Melissa's Story

Melissa and Karen wake up each day to the drone of the Islamic call to prayer. The muezzin's penetrating cry toward Allah rends the morning air and demands the attention of all, those faithful and those not. Full submission to Allah is at the heart of the call.

Though it seemed eerie at first to their uninitiated ears, Melissa and Karen quickly learned to hear the heart of this call, and as they reflected upon their own lives, nothing about their regular routine seemed to call so passionately for their devotion to God. Thus began a morning pattern of kneeling in prayer to God at the sound of the muezzin's plea. They pray together:

Oh, the depth of the riches of the wisdom and knowledge of God!

How unsearchable his judgments,

and his paths beyond tracing out!

"Who has known the mind of the Lord?

Or who has been his counselor?"

"Who has ever given to God,

that God should repay him?"

For from him and through him and to him are all things.

To him be the glory forever! Amen. (Rom 11:33-36)

From this memorized section of Romans, they move each day to a time of intercession for Muslims. A wall map highlights Muslim regions around the world; each continent is prayed over on a specific day of the week. Each country of the continent is prayed for by name. They have learned the names of certain Islamic government leaders and pray for them as well.

Sunday is reserved for prayer about their own lives—prayer that God will keep them fit for the work of the kingdom. Melissa's favorite Sunday prayer is to read through the announcement of Jesus' coming in Isaiah 61. She asks God to make her sensitive to the needs of her new Islamic friends, able to reflect the tenderness and complete love of Christ. Karen goes for the caffeine-no-cream passage (in her words) of Philippians 2:6-11. She asks God to make her a pure and loving servant, capable of following in the footsteps of Jesus.

It has been two and a half years now since these two boarded a United Airlines flight from New York's La Guardia Airport for London. They are an unlikely pair—Melissa a journalism major from Columbia University, Karen a religious studies major from Gordon College.

They met at a large mission conference called Urbana 87. It's not as though they couldn't have avoided each other, given that more than 15,000 other students were attending Urbana 87. Apparently God had plans. Karen and Melissa were assigned to the same small study/prayer group. By the end of the five-day convention the two of them had discovered a common interest—Islam.

Karen about Melissa: "She scared me at first. All this talk about sexism in Christianity and the parochial view of American Christians in relation to the rest of the world. I remember one conversation we had about politics. Melissa said the basic difference between South Africa and the United States was that the U.S. had learned to be more sophisticated in its racism! I was really angry that night. I prayed with my roommate that God would give me grace to be nice to Melissa the next morning at the small-group Bible study."

Melissa about Karen: "Yes, she did get real defensive. But then, I can't say I was exercising the gift of diplomacy. Karen represented so much about my past that I resented—conservative Christianity with all the trappings. But I couldn't get away from her genuine care for me as a person. I'd be ready for a good fight the next day . . . and she would be ready to ask how well I had slept."

"God used the world to bring us together," says Melissa. "I guess that's how it works in our walk with Jesus. As we look beyond ourselves, we get better at living the Christian life."

Karen echoes the sentiment: "How could we honestly claim to love Muslims if we didn't even love each other? God brought his global concern right into our Bible study group. The idea of loving the world became very specific as Melissa and I stared at each other across the circle."

Neither of these women was forming specific plans to work with each other. They were simply building a new friendship. Over the next year several letters went between them and they agreed to "the nutty idea" of getting together to celebrate the first anniversary of meeting at Urbana. It turned out to be a powerful week and both of them say God called them that Christmas to become missionary partners to the Islamic world. "You can't imagine the feeling between us. It was the Blues Brothers all over. We were on a mission from God."

During the next eighteen months Karen and Melissa looked for very specific guidance from God. They went through a summer of training, raised financial support from friends and churches, moved to London for a year of language training as interns with a progressive mission agency. With a large Islamic presence in England supported by more than 400 mosques, London made a perfect place to get familiar with their calling, before going to a Muslim country.

But after language school they stayed on in London. God had given them strong friendships there with expatriate Muslim women, and they just couldn't walk away from those people. Neither of them is sure how future plans will shape up, but both are sure their future is tied up with people devoted to Allah.

And so, after morning prayers, Melissa goes downstairs to the corner cafe where she gets her daily intake of newspapers, Karen works on a correspondence course in theology, and by mid-morning they hit the streets of London.

Racism in North America and South Africa: Ricardo's Story

Ricardo lives in Soweto. His morning routine begins with an early prayer meeting of several pastors in the region. They have been meeting every day for more than a year now, to ask God to give them wisdom and love during the traumatic days facing their country. This exceptional gathering of ministers from several different denominations has often served as the healing place for men and women who suffer discouragement and loss of hope in the difficult work of reconciliation. Beyond the denominational differences are the ethnic differences. In a country that officially separates people along ethnic lines, this prayer group serves notice that the kingdom of God transcends racial barriers and in fact works hard to break down racial barriers.

Ricardo is not unaware of the privilege of peeking in on this group every day. His letters to his college friends still reflect the sense of awe he has after eight months on assignment. "Do you ever get the feeling you were peeking in on the oval office by accident? And there was the president. He notices you and winks permission to let you slip in and eavesdrop on high-level conversations."

Ricardo's journey to Soweto began with a spring-break trip to an inner-city ministry in Los Angeles. "No question God wanted me there. I was looking for some short-term adventure; I really wanted my break to count for something." His girlfriend, Jennifer, had spent the previous summer working there and challenged Ricardo to let God reach him through a slice of life that was outside his experience.

Jennifer's stories about her summer in Los Angeles had Ricardo well prepared for the spring-break outreach program. What he didn't expect was his reaction to the conflict between the police and local residents. "It was just crazy. I kept asking myself, 'Is this really America?' Something in my upbringing had taught me to believe that police brutality happens 'over there.' I was absolutely shocked to witness the animosity between these two groups."

The spring break was over too soon. After finals, Ricardo returned for the entire summer. His search for understanding was genuine and earnest. A robust prayer life developed, as well as a steady diet of reading regarding racism and justice. "I think it's fair to say I experienced a 'mini' second conversion that summer. I learned that God is a God of justice. I cannot just accept a personal salvation that stops at the personal benefits of forgiveness and heaven. God's love extends to my relationships. I realized I must accept the public demands of the gospel on my life if I want the private benefits."

The summer brought three important experiences to Ricardo. The first was a robbery that cleaned out all his expensive summer trappings. "I was furious! I mean, my camera, my CD player, my notebook computer. Who are they to do that to me?"

As the staff helped Ricardo work through the robbery, he was confronted with his own feelings of racism. "Those" people were all a different color in his mind. And in time he realized he was accepting the convenient category of race to describe the people who had robbed him. "I realized how personal racism is. God had to work me over on that one. I suppose I was proud of myself for deciding to return to the inner city—you know, it was a real holy thing to do. And now here I was without my favorite possessions because 'they' took them from me." Ricardo's faith was required to go further than in any previous experience. He was tempted to forgo the hard work of listening to God through the personal trial, but in the end faith triumphed.

The second key event came early in the summer. Ricardo attended the funeral of one of the neighborhood kids killed by a drug overdose. "It was as though my understanding of life just suddenly entered a new category. There I was, looking at the grieving mother and brother. This was real. Nothing theoretical about it. If you can hear God speak, I'd say he spoke to me at that funeral. I rededicated myself to God at a funeral. I told God, 'I want to live a real life. I really want my life to make a difference in other people's lives.'"

Before the summer was over, the third major impact came in the form of a guest speaker from South Africa. The pastor from Soweto challenged the summer staff to consider God's global call, to think about justice as a global problem. That's all Ricardo remembers hearing. "I went to the altar. I said, 'Yes, Lord.' It was that simple—and now here I am in Soweto."

Regarding Jennifer: "We've been dating for four years now. I would love to be married but she has lots more to see before settling down." Jennifer is currently working in a refugee camp in northern Thailand and thinks her next stop will be Amsterdam. Prior to Thailand she was in Russia. "We're sorting out God's call on our lives. My friends think I'm wild. My defense is to point to Jennifer! I know I'm where I belong right now and you couldn't tear me away from this place."

Nighttime Prayer in Hong Kong: LaShana's Story

LaShana sits on the deck as late as she can each night. "If you look at the world only in daylight you miss half the story," she offers. Across the Hong Kong harbor blink a million lights, lights that in her mind represent a million stories of hope, aspiration and pain. Her opening journal entry from her first night here a month ago reads, "Each light is calling out to Jesus, like a lantern on a ship lost at sea in a storm. Jesus can hold the pain of each light in his heart. I pray that I will be able to absorb the pain of just one."

Some start their day with prayer. LaShana ends it in prayer. She believes that God guides us in our prayers, and so she sits on the deck as long as she senses the nudging of the Holy Spirit. She fixes her gaze on one light at a time and prays as specifically as she can. Her evening sessions typically run from ten p.m. till about three a.m. "This is the heart of my ministry. I've met a lot of missionaries who are working directly with people each day, and the truth is, I feel like their silent supporter. Prayer is my calling," says LaShana.

"One night while praying over a couple of lights, I was overcome with a deep and penetrating sorrow. I just cried and cried and cried. And when I ran out of energy to cry, it felt like someone else started crying through me."

At noon the next day she had her "breakfast" and, as is her pattern, her daily quiet time. Her reading for that day focused on the shortest and most . penetrating verse in the Bible: "Jesus wept" (Jn 11:35). "I learned something new about Jesus that day. Think about this—he carries the pain of society so close to his heart that he still cries. He really does feel the pain. From two thousand years ago we have the record of his tears as he looked over Jerusalem. Today he cries over the great city of Hong Kong. It's good for me to know I'm not alone. In fact, it's good for me to know that my tears are really Jesus' tears."

Most of LaShana's afternoon is taken with personal affairs. For the last couple weeks she has been able to arrange a private tour each day, for an hour, of some part of Hong Kong. Missionaries take her around and show her something about the city that will help her pray. After dinner she joins three other missionaries who do a "Joshua Walk" every night. This idea is taken from the Old Testament record of Joshua and his soldiers walking around the city of Jericho seven times to claim it for Yahweh. "I learned the idea on a short-term mission trip I was on in Egypt. Every day a couple of us would team up together and walk around a certain block of the city. We were claiming that block and all its residents for the kingdom. Everyone on the team was expected to do this. Now I'm doing it here in Hong Kong." Each walk lasts about an hour. Then LaShana takes the ferry across the bay and catches a shuttle up the hill to her deck where she begins her nighttime ministry of intercession.

When will her ministry end in Hong Kong? "I don't know. I was in Egypt for three months with a team. The schedule was planned out ahead of time. This round is different. I'll stay until the nudge is there to move on. I'm really fortunate to have supporters who believe in the ministry of prayer. I guess they are the real silent partners in missions."

LaShana's life of prayer is barely three years old. It started when she was invited to a "Concert of Prayer" in her home town of Jackson, Mississippi. The entire evening was spent in worship and prayer. The prayer time was divided between prayers for God to work in the United States—to save the family, guide the government, break down the barriers that divide ethnic groups, and end the scourge of drugs. The second half of the prayer time was for world evangelization—prayers for people all around the world who have not heard of God's love.

It was during this night of prayer that LaShana heard a new term: "Unreached Peoples." The leader of the Concert explained that perhaps as many as two billion people belong to cultural groups where the gospel is barely known. These are the Unreached Peoples. LaShana felt immediately drawn to pray for these people. At the end of the evening she asked for more information and was steered in the direction of a group that leads prayer tours to unreached areas. This was her link to Egypt, and within the year she left for Cairo. By the end of the trip LaShana was sure God was calling her to prayer as a lifestyle. She immediately set out to raise regular financial support, and in less than a year she was in Hong Kong, making it her new home.

"I left a really great job to do this. My parents thought I was absolutely crazy and I think they are right. You have to be a little crazy to follow the call of city lights on another continent. Watch out, world!"

God planted in each of us the natural desire to howl at the moon. Perhaps our moon is the landscape of lights in the Hong Kong harbor, the cry of a muezzin's prayer at dawn, the song of a tropical river dancing around rocks at dusk. It's the call of the wild. And whatever form the call of the wild takes as it grabs hold of us, there is something in each of us that screams against the idea of living a "normal" life. Deep down inside, we resist the notion of a routine existence—getting out of bed, going to work, recuperating from the day, going to bed, getting out of bed again the next morning. *Boring.*

History is replete with stories of men and women who howled at the moon—climbing impossible peaks, jumping off cliffs with wings attached to their arms, searching for the source of the Nile, shipping out to find the new world, plunging the depth of the ocean to trace its contour, capturing the wind for power, sitting in a rocket ship on the way to the moon. We're still reaching to settle Mars, squinting to discover the basic unit of life, looking for heaven, attempting to perfect the body and prolong our years. All diseases are simply a challenge to conquer, "virtual sex" is within reach and world peace is on the drawing-board.

Howling. It's a God-given gift. Not that we always direct our wild inner selves toward noble purposes. In fact, too much of history is the record of men and women who destroyed others and their environment with the force of a powerful, uncontrolled river that cuts its way through the earth without regard for the life in its pathway.

But there is a call of the wild that stirs deep from the heart of God. You read some of those stories at the beginning of this chapter—stories of men and women who heard the cry of the world and were stirred to action. Something inside them simply answered yes. Indeed, the call of the wild is most often broadcast through the pain of society.

And we have one who went before us, one who heard the call of the wild, one who said yes. The prophet Isaiah, years before the advent of that one, predicts his response to the call:

The Spirit of the Sovereign LORD is on me,
because the LORD has anointed me
to preach good news to the poor.
He has sent me to bind up the brokenhearted,
to proclaim freedom for the captives
and release for the prisoners,
to proclaim the year of the LORD's favor
and the day of vengeance of our God,
to comfort all who mourn,
and provide for those who grieve in Zion—
to bestow on them a crown of beauty
instead of ashes,
the oil of gladness
instead of mourning,
and a garment of praise
instead of a spirit of despair. (Is 61:1-3)

Jesus heard the call of the world. It took him down a path called Calvary, and there he hung his response. If you have heard that call, you are in good company.

2
Romancing the Globe

When we come into a relationship with Christ we are, above all else, called into an affair of the heart. The great commandment "Love the Lord your God with all your heart, soul, mind and strength" is the substance of our life.

To be sure, there are other biblical notions in addition to love that help us understand what it means to follow Christ. We have teachings about obedience, duty, service and obligation, to name a few. Discipleship includes all of these. And when Christ called us into relationship, we were called into a lifestyle that includes all of these. We have to think of discipleship as *a way of living that continually takes us closer to the heart of God.* The closer we come to God, the more we discover what's important to him. And then we fashion our lives after this enlarged understanding.

The Story of the Talents
In Matthew 25:14-30, Jesus tells his disciples the parable of a master who

handed out talents (money) to each of his workers. The master left town and told each of them to work for the increase of his kingdom while he was gone. The first two were industrious and immediately set about finding ways to increase the talents that were entrusted to them. The third, however, was fearful that he would not do a good job with the talent he had been given. So, rather than ruining it, he buried it where it would be safe until the master's return.

When the master came back he asked for an accounting of the talents. The first two had doubled what they received—the first from five talents to ten, the second from two talents to four. Each of these workers were rewarded and their responsibilities were greatly increased. They showed themselves capable of caring for the master's concerns.

The third worker dug up his talent and returned it to the master unharmed. The master was not very understanding. In fact, he instructed his servants to "throw that worthless servant outside, into the darkness."

Apparently fear does not rate in God's mind as a reason to disengage ourselves from the work of the kingdom. There is a degree to which we have to view our talents as God's property. We do not have the right to do with them as we wish. We must use them as *he* wishes.

The idea here, of course, is that the gospel is not a private possession. It is a public trust. Jesus was using this parable to teach his disciples that he desires his kingdom to increase. When we benefit personally from the good news, the gospel, we are in fact entrusted with "talents" (including both the information we've received about the gospel and the skills built into us which can help us communicate that information). It is now our duty to put those talents to work for the benefit of others. This is something that is central to the nature of God.

The closer we draw to God, the more we will discover one whose heart is always going out, always looking for ways to increase the members of the kingdom. We are left with the question: How will I allow God to use my talents for the sake of others? How will the salvation that I have experienced become available to others through the way I live my life? And it helps if we turn the question around: How does my life hoard the good news? What barriers in my life prevent God from using my talents to the benefit of others?

The Good Samaritan

As Luke 10:25-37 records it, a religious person came to Jesus to ask how he could inherit eternal life. When Jesus asked him what the Law said about that, he could give the answer verbatim.

But Jesus pushes him beyond the letter of the law and puts in front of him the requirements of the spirit of the law: You must love your neighbor. Rather than getting specific on "How do I love my neighbor?" this man asks Jesus, "And who is my neighbor?" Perhaps he was avoiding the answer. Perhaps he wanted the legalistic boundaries of "Okay, who actually fits into that category?"

Christ begins to tell him a story about a man who is accosted by some robbers. Not only do they steal his belongings, but they beat him severely and leave him at the side of the road (probably to die). The first person to walk by is a priest—a religious leader of the day whom we would expect to be faithful to all the requirements of the law (including the duty to help a person in distress). He does not even stop to inspect the man's wounds. Rather, he hastens past to get on with his duties as a religious leader. A second person, a Levite, also walks by. The Levites were entrusted with the work of caring for the synagogue. We would expect this man to fulfill the requirements of the law. But he too passes by the wounded man.

Then along comes the Samaritan. He stops by the victim, transports him to a local motel, dresses his wounds, pays for his keep—and returns later to settle the bill! What makes this story exceptional at one level is that Jesus is using religious leaders of the day to make his point. It was no doubt credible to Jews of the day that religious leaders could ignore the needs of people around them and still fulfill their religious duties. And the man in the ditch was "one of us."

But what makes the story even more exceptional is that a Samaritan is the one who actually cares for the victim. The Samaritans were known as "half-breeds." They were mixed-blood Jews in whose lineage the purity of the race had been compromised. As a consequence they were despised by the "pure" Jews who felt racially superior. The person listening to Jesus' story certainly would not have expected a Samaritan to help a distressed Jew. Instead, he would have expected this despised man to mutter under his breath, "Good. I wish they would *all* fall by the wayside." Rather than seeing the harsh reaction of a Samaritan, we see the cold response of the religious leaders.

Jesus wants his questioner to know that being religious does not fulfill the concerns that lie close to the heart of God. At the end of the story of the Good Samaritan, we learn Jesus' main point. The question is not so much "Who is my neighbor?" as "Are you a good neighbor?" A good neighbor is one who actively looks out for the needs of others—who, in fact, is able to overcome barriers of race and nationality, or whatever they may be, in order to be a good neighbor. There is no legalistic way to fulfill this requirement. It is a way of life that reflects the heart of God.

We are confronted here with more questions about our lifestyle. In what ways do I ignore the needs of those about me? In what ways do I allow the comfort of my religious lifestyle to lull me to sleep, fooling me into thinking I am living a life that reflects the heart of God? What kinds of prejudices or barriers keep me from freely responding to certain kinds of people?

The Substance of the Law

Jesus takes us further down this road with a more difficult picture. In Matthew 23 he becomes openly hostile with the Pharisees, calling them unflattering names such as a brood of vipers and whitewashed tombstones. He says the argument he has with them is that they keep producing religious people rather than producing people who accept the concerns of God. It was not that the Pharisees were unconcerned about others—in fact they traveled over hills and across oceans to make converts—but that upon achieving this goal they made the poor convert "twice as much a son of hell" as they themselves were (v. 15). Jesus' accusations are strongly stated. Not very diplomatic.

The problem, Jesus explains, is that these Pharisees have been careful to follow the legalistic concept of the law—attending synagogue, giving tithes and offerings—but they have neglected "the more important matters of the law—justice, mercy and faithfulness" (v. 23). The Pharisees have managed to be so focused on the wrong concept of following God that they "strain out a gnat but swallow a camel" (v. 24).

This criticism was not new to them. Much of the Old Testament is a record of God's argument with Israel. Somehow the people of Israel—the community that was supposed to be the living example of God's heart—were able to ignore the compassionate nature of their Lord.

A classic summary of that argument is found in Isaiah 58 where God tells Israel that they have been careful to keep the legalistic rules but have missed the substance. In verses 6-7, 9-10, he asks them a series of questions:

Is not this the kind of fasting I have chosen:
to loose the chains of injustice
    and untie the cords of the yoke,
to set the oppressed free
    and break every yoke?
Is it not to share your food with the hungry
    and to provide the poor wanderer with shelter—
when you see the naked, to clothe him,
    and not to turn away from your own flesh and blood? . . .
If you do away with the yoke of oppression,
    with the pointing finger and malicious talk,
and if you spend yourselves in behalf of the hungry
    and satisfy the needs of the oppressed,
then your light will rise in the darkness,
    and your night will become like the noonday.

As we draw close to the heart of God we discover that God truly does care about people's plight. God is telling Israel that they cannot claim to follow Yahweh if their lifestyle does not reflect that caring. If they want their "light to shine" for others to see, they must live a caring lifestyle.

This picture offered by God in Matthew 23 and Isaiah 58 leaves us with some personal questions: How does my life go beyond doctrinal positions to a caring lifestyle? Do I feel secure in my beliefs without sensing the heart of God's concerns? In what ways does my light shine for others?

The End of Time

In Matthew 25, just a couple of chapters after Jesus labels the Pharisees as vipers, he describes a picture of the end of time. Jesus tells his listeners that on that last day, a large group of people will be surprised that Jesus denies them entrance into heaven. On earth they called him "Lord" and they went so far as to do miraculous deeds in Jesus' name. But Jesus claims he does not recognize them. He orders them cast into outer darkness—and the reason he offers is that they didn't feed him when he was hungry, they didn't give him water to drink when he was thirsty, they didn't visit him when he was sick and in prison, and they didn't provide him with clothes when he was naked.

Can we conclude by this that we earn our way into heaven by good works? No, the Scriptures are absolutely clear that we receive the gift of forgiveness by grace alone. But the Scriptures do not allow the possibility of being Christian and also ignoring those in need. Apparently Jesus is suggesting that our works, though not making us Christian, show that we are Christian. The message to the Old Testament Israelites, to believers in the New Testament and to us today is identical: *We cannot claim the identity of God if we do not follow his ways.* We are ambassadors to the world, not independent operators. And as ambassadors of Jesus Christ we must faithfully represent his concerns to society.

Again, there are a couple of questions we must ask ourselves: What message does our lifestyle portray to the world? Would Jesus recognize us in heaven? We cannot sidestep these critical issues if God carefully placed them in the Scriptures for our understanding.

Everyone Is Welcome

Jesus tells his disciples a parable (Mt 22:1-14) about a man who prepares a banquet for prominent guests. On the evening of the dinner, none of them show. They all have reasons, of course, and those reasons largely center around business concerns or relationships. The host does not let this deter him. He tells his servants, "Go to the street corners and invite to the banquet anyone you find" (v. 9). He wants everyone to know that the banquet is open to whoever chooses to come.

This parable was directed once again to the religious leaders of the day. He was telling them through a story line that they had rejected the Messiah. The invitation to the banquet was turned down. And now the banquet table was fast filling up with people who were not Jewish. The message to these leaders was that the kingdom is much larger than the population of Israelites. God is, as it were, racing back and forth over the face of the earth, in the highways and byways, inviting any and all to become members of his kingdom.

The parables of the lost sheep and the lost coin (Lk 15:3-10) tell us of the same far-reaching love. Jesus tells us that if a shepherd owns a hundred sheep, he will not be satisfied to see that ninety-nine are in the fold. The fact that one is missing is too much to ignore. The shepherd leaves the ninety-nine in the fold and goes into the hills to search for the one which is lost. Similarly, he tells the story of a woman who loses one of her ten gold coins. She becomes obsessed with the loss and thoroughly cleans the house until the lost coin is found. She is so jubilant that she calls her friends over and throws a massive party to celebrate the find. The message to us is clear enough. This same love is taught in the story of the prodigal son (Lk 15:11-31). Jesus waits for all those outside the house of God to come home. And when they do, he will kill the fattened calf and throw a celebration that even befuddles the angels.

When we accept the grace of Jesus into our lives, we have been touched by a love that is constantly searching for more people to bless. And when we accept that grace, we are accepting the duty that goes with it—the requirement to bring others into the same love we have found.

The book of Revelation gives us a picture of how far God's love extends. We are told that at the final banquet in heaven—that great dinner which Jesus told his disciples would be the next time he would celebrate Communion with them—every tribe, tongue and nation will be represented. God's love will have been successful in its desire to extend its arms to all the world. Every single society will be represented at the wonderful celebration at the end of time. This hopeful picture fits squarely with our understanding of a God who does not want anyone to perish (2 Pet 3:9).

The theme of love is the single most important thread that weaves its way through the Scriptures. God is actually wooing all of the world's people to himself. He is like the lover who is restless to win the loved one over. And God's love is global. It extends to every corner of society, every language, every individual. We could say that God is romancing the globe. Those of us who have found the love of Jesus are called to become partners in this great romance story.

Love Is All You Need

The Beatles were right in their understanding of the pervasive role of love. Sure, they may not have thoroughly understood the nature of true love, but none of us really do. Listen to the poetry, music, novels and folklore of any society and you will quickly discover that the subject of love dominates the landscape. Tragically, the church has often denied the legitimacy of the art forms crying out for love. Too often we have mistaken these passionate renderings as nothing more than sexual perversion. We have missed the point of most of them and, more seriously, we have missed the opportunity to connect with the desires and needs of people outside the church.

The Scriptures tell us that we were conceived in love. We are not some cosmic project of God that makes good discussion material in celestial museums. We are the children of God. And we are meant to catch the intimate overtones in the Bible that we are *conceived* in the heart of God in a fashion that is not much different to our earthly conception in the intimacy of sexual intercourse.

We cannot miss how central this theme is to our lives. Our walk with Christ is confusing, sometimes, because we have not learned our true identity. We have equated God with a cosmic military leader who intrudes upon our lives like a distant parental figure in a segment of *Star Trek*. Our duty is to give unquestioned obedience to this Being—if for no other reason than that he is bigger and more powerful than we are. Clearly, this is a ridiculous portrait of God. But if we think carefully about the language we use to describe our relationship with God, this picture may not be too far off the mark.

God does call us to full obedience. But we cannot understand the heart of

God through the language of obedience and duty. And we certainly cannot understand who we are as created beings of the loving God.

Our constant search for love is no deviant pursuit. It is perfectly descriptive of how God made us. From the day we are conceived we experience the warmth and security of the womb. Our entrance into the world is marked by the constant attention of parents who cuddle, rock and stroke us. And breastfeeding is clearly not just a physiological function for the infant, but a warm nurturing experience as well. As we grow older, our close circle of relationships, the family, is meant to be our source of security. And as we continue to grow in years, we look for friends to fill our relationship needs. That often progresses to the point of marriage, sexual intimacy and through the whole cycle to the point where we in turn are conceiving in love.

Humans are made for community. That is how God designed us. We need each other, and the singers' cry of wanting to know what love is and where to find it is nothing less than the wail of all the world. If you find yourself crying the same words, you are simply displaying the fingerprints of God upon your soul. And that cry will be with all of us until the day we experience the final and perfecting stage of our lives—complete union with the one who made us in love.

This fact of love and longing is the basis of what we call Christian community. The church is that intimate gathering of Christians whose longings are being met both in the person and promises of Christ and in the family of Christ. We'll come back to that theme later in the book.

The Pain of God

God lives with pain. He carries with him the burden of the parent who is separated from his children, the burden of the lover who is cut off from the loved one. It is a perverted view of perfection that would tell us God does not "feel." Indeed, it is precisely because God is perfect that he feels pain. We could say that he feels pain perfectly.

The Garden of Eden is the beginning of the drama of pain. There God has fellowship with those he created in love, and there Adam and Eve are able to walk in total honesty and intimacy with each other and with God. Their need for each other is described to us through the story of creation. Adam could not satisfy his need for companionship through his friendship with the animals, nor, in fact, through his friendship with God. He needed another person, and so God created Eve.

Tragically, Satan is able to destroy this intimate picture of love and community. We cannot understand all the specifics that led to this great drama—that will come one day as we sit at Jesus' feet—but we do know that both humans and heaven have been longing ever since. As Adam and Eve are banished from the Garden to live a life of separation and loneliness, the great Lover enters a personal journey of wooing all creation back to him. The Song of Songs is a poetic account of the Lover and the Beloved. The longing for spring (the end of the effects of the Fall) is expressed in the language of desire and searching:

> See! The winter is past;
> > the rains are over and gone.
> Flowers appear on the earth;·
> > the season of singing has come,
> the cooing of doves
> > is heard in our land.
> The fig tree forms its early fruit;
> > the blossoming vines spread their fragrance.
> Arise, come, my darling;
> > my beautiful one, come with me. . . .
>
> All night long on my bed
> I looked for the one my heart loves;
> I looked for him but did not find him.
> I will get up now and go about the city,
> > through its streets and squares;
> I will search for the one my heart loves.
> > So I looked for him but did not find him.
> The watchmen found me

as they made their rounds in the city.
"Have you seen the one my heart loves?"
Scarcely had I passed them
when I found the one my heart loves.
I held him and would not let him go
till I had brought him to my mother's house,
to the room of the one who conceived me.
(Song 2:11-13; 3:1-4)

The prophet Jeremiah continues the image of a lover for us when describing God's feelings toward Israel for going astray.

I remember the devotion of your youth,
how as a bride you loved me
and followed me through the desert,
through a land not sown. (Jer 2:2)

And now Israel is taken with other gods. It is not as though they have simply changed their doctrinal orientation. No, they are being unfaithful to their bridegroom. Several passages in Jeremiah describe Israel as a spouse who has become a prostitute, willing to lie down with anyone who requests her love. But God, the pained lover, is willing to take her back if she will agree to it.

God's longing is full of the language of pain.

One of the great missionary passages from the New Testament, "Ask the Lord of the harvest, therefore, to send out workers into his harvest field" (Mt 9:38) comes as the result of contact with human pain. Jesus, as described in Matthew 9, is walking through towns and villages, healing every form of disease and sickness. The press of human need is intense. Finally, the Scriptures tell us, Jesus is "overcome with sorrow," and then gives his call to prayer.

We see this same compassion, this same pain, as Jesus is walking toward the city of Jerusalem on one occasion (Lk 19:41). The sight of that great city moves him; his heart feels the impact of the tragedy—his separation from the children of Israel. His mind goes back to the Garden of Eden, no doubt, and then journeys through the annals of time as four thousand years of broken relationship crush against his heart.

And Jesus wept over the city.

This is our God who feels the pain perfectly. This is our God who resolved to reconcile the broken relationship, who went to the point of giving up his life to restore our love. We have to understand Calvary in the context of God's pain. There was no requirement that Jesus had to go to Calvary. He could have obliterated all of human life and begun anew. But we were not a project—we are his loved ones. And as he pressed toward Jerusalem, against his disciples' advice, Jesus bore the tragedy of Eden like a thorn that pierces the heart. Finally, in his moment of triumph he was able to cry, "It is finished," and he died from the exhaustion of his pursuit.

For three days he lay in the grave—perhaps an extended sabbath where our God rested from the work of restoring creation to himself—and then he left the grave, triumphant, with the message that whoever wants to may come to him and he will grant them victory over the grave and a place in paradise—where there will be no more sorrows, no more tears, no more pain. Only pleasures forevermore.

And now God continues to move across the face of the earth wooing us into his family of love. He wills that none should perish. One "lost sheep" is too many! And even though many reject him, he is tireless in his endeavor to bring all of us back to our rightful home.

Our Pain

There is no better news for us than that God feels our pain. The gospel is intensely personal in this regard. There is no heartache, sorrow, disappointment, abuse or loss which God does not feel. Somehow God is able to absorb the great swaths of pain that afflict the entire globe, but in his sovereign nature he also absorbs the individual story of each of our lives.

We see this fact in the Scriptures. God was careful to see to it that Scripture recorded, for our understanding, the encounters Jesus had with individuals—Zacchaeus, the woman at the well, blind Bartimaeus, the woman with excessive bleeding, Lazarus, the centurion's daughter, Mary, Martha, Nicodemus. All of these people lived with their own pain—some physical, some emotional, some spiritual, some a complex mix of all three. God met them at their point of need.

Personal Pain: Dan's Story

I (Dan) have experienced this in my own life. When I was fifteen, I was arrested for driving without a license. They took me to the county jail and put me in a cell, slamming the door behind me. I turned around and saw my brother, Frank. I didn't expect a family reunion. Naturally, I used my one telephone call to call home. My father refused to speak to me, and he wouldn't let my mother, either. Dad had told me that I would get in trouble for driving without a license, and if I did, not to call on him.

When I was twelve, I was in the outhouse we had behind our old country home, again with Frank. He was smoking, and so I decided I wanted to puff on a cigarette. As I went to the house, my father, who was in the woodshed, noticed me. He said, "You've been smoking!" I responded very rudely. He ordered me to go in my bedroom immediately and take down my jeans. "I'll go in the bedroom, but I won't take down my Levis," I said.

Dad later came to my bedroom, took off his two-inch belt and began to thrash me. He said repeatedly, "Promise me you'll never smoke again!" And I said, "I'll promise you I'm going to learn how to smoke!" We continued until he finally gave up in exhaustion. I thumbed a ride to town, found a friend who smoked and started my smoking career.

That same year, at twelve, I had my first drink at a bar and began drinking in a substantial way. I specialized in truancy as a student in high school. In my tenth-grade year, I was in school probably a total of forty-five days. I quit high school so many times I lost count.

When I was fourteen, I got a letter from Dad. I was in Florida then, visiting Frank and his new bride and baby. The substance of the letter focused on my responsibility to pay back the money I had borrowed from Dad to go on that trip, and how I was going to pay it back. But at the bottom of the letter, it said, "Love, Dad." My dad loved me! He had never used those words before. He loved me.

That piece of paper became very precious to me. I have no idea whether I paid that debt back, but I kept that paper in my wallet until I wore it out.

I never seemed to please my missionary dad. I'm not proud to tell you I hated my father during my teenage years. My parents were godly people who were committed to fulfilling the Great Commission. The verse Matthew 6:33—"Seek first his kingdom and his righteousness, and all these things will be given to you as well"—meant to them, among other things, that the Tibetans, the people they served as missionaries overseas, came first. In the U.S., it meant child evangelism classes came first. "And all these things will be given to you" meant that God would look after the children. I was last and knew it.

I despised my father's frugality. I resented his severe discipline. I was embarrassed by my parents' lifestyle. I felt desperately insecure. I was broken—what today we would call a dysfunctional teenager.

What is this dysfunctionality business? All of us, after all, start out fragile and experience some type of abuse. But a dysfunctional home is one characterized by rigid rules and a lack of trust, where feelings are something that you keep under control. I understood it to mean that I was to "stuff" my feelings. There was no open communication, especially regarding painful subjects. I was desperately insecure (that's often a characteristic of a dysfunctional home). There's perfectionism sometimes, and denial. Sometimes there's physical abuse and sexual abuse. There was none of that in my home, nor substance abuse.

Does any of this apply to you today? Are you in pain? I believe that perhaps fifty percent or more of the young people reading this have grown up in a single-parent family. They know something of the brokenness I'm describing. It may be different in your case. Tragically, the number of single-parent homes is on the rise in North America. Of course, there aren't any perfect families.

But is there hope for the dysfunctional, the broken? Is healing available to us? Or is pain a permanent condition?

Let's look briefly at three verses of Scripture. In 2 Corinthians 12:9 Paul tells of hearing the words, "My grace is sufficient for you, for my power is made perfect in weakness." It is *my* strength, the Lord said, that's made perfect in *your* weakness. Then, 1 Corinthians 1:27 says, "God chose the weak things of the world to shame the strong." And 2 Corinthians 1:4 says that God "comforts us in all our troubles." He knows exactly how troubled and weak you are. And he will help you.

In the late sixties, we were missionaries with Wycliffe Bible Translators in Papua New Guinea. One day as my wife swept the floor, she knocked off a precious pot, and it broke in many pieces. It was the only souvenir we had of our honeymoon. Both of us wept. In a lot of ways that broken pot with its pieces is like my life.

I tried to put the pot back together, as best I could.

In West China, where I was born among the Tibetan people, in every village there is a person that I'll refer to as the tinker man. He has a little bell, and when people hear the bell, they know they can bring out their broken items, like that pot. They bring all the slivers and every little piece. He takes them and pieces it back together. Actually, the joints are stronger than it was before it broke. It's amazing.

As a teenager in 1958, I was living with my parents on the campus of Cornell University. My parents began looking after an elderly professor, Walter Wilcox. He was ninety-seven when we met him. My mother led him to the Lord when he was 102. Walter Wilcox was a man of ideas. He still read a book a day. A Webster's unabridged dictionary was next to the table. And so I entered the world of ideas. I wasn't used to ideas. Nobody talked to me about ideas. They talked to me about important things like how long my hair was, how tight my Levis were and how much grease I had under my fingernails. Professor Wilcox never said to me that I was intelligent. I felt intelligent around him. It was the grace of God.

I finished high school, majoring in shop. I didn't have many opportunities available for college, unless somebody granted some grace. I wrote to Bryan College, a Christian school, at my parents' encouragement. My letter went along these lines: "Dear Mr. President, I'm not a Christian. I smoke and drink. I noticed you've got a lot of rules. I don't promise to keep them, but I'll try. I want an education, and besides, I'm a missionary kid." (I figured if you've got a trump card, you might as well play it.)

Dr. Mercer, the president of Bryan College, responded by inviting me to come. As soon as I arrived on the campus, he invited me into his office. *I'm in trouble already,* I thought. He said, "Young man, you and I know a great deal about your past, don't we?" I said, "Yes, sir, we do." He said, "I want you to know that not another person on this campus knows anything about your background. Why don't you allow the beautiful person God made you to be to flourish in this setting? Don't let the past encumber you. Get the help that you need. You probably need some." I had never received or understood that kind of grace before. When I went out of that office, I had a lot of things to think about. He gave me grace. More pieces back into that broken pot.

I experienced love from some of the students there at Bryan. While there had been Christian love around me before, in my home as I grew up, I had not been receptive to it. But I received it at Bryan somehow, and the wall that I had raised to protect me from Christians and their God began to crumble. One morning after chapel, I committed my heart to Christ, at the encouragement of my roommate. More grace; more pieces back into that broken pot.

Shelby, my spouse, came from a broken home. Her father left the home when she was thirteen. But Shelby and I committed ourselves to one another—to trust one another. I don't know where we got such an idea, but it was a good one. And Shelby granted me the gift of unconditional love. What a precious gift. And so I received more peace, more grace.

I transferred from Bryan to Cornell University. At Bryan, I had been involved in the Student Foreign Mission Fellowship (now InterVarsity Missions Fellowship), and began to pray for missionaries. I became more and more interested in doing that. When I transferred to Cornell, I got actively involved in the InterVarsity chapter there. It was very influential in my life. And because my parents were still living on the campus, I had lunch with them nearly every day. And you know, I spent a lot of time talking to my dad—and listening to him. I was surprised to find he was actually a wise and caring man. The eyes of faith opened my eyes to the beautiful people my parents were. They're with the Lord now.

But I had to reconcile myself to my dad. One day I felt under conviction, and I went to him and said, "Dad, would you forgive me for my rebellious spirit? Would you forgive me for the way I've disgraced the family name? Would you forgive me for not submitting to your authority? I feel robbed of the benefit of your spiritual leadership in my life because of that. Would you forgive me?" And he did. More grace, precious grace.

In 1970, we were on our first furlough from Papua New Guinea. It was a difficult furlough. We nearly lost one of our children through illness, and we hadn't experienced the renewal in our spirits that we needed. But we got some teaching toward the end of our furlough regarding the biblical call to reconciliation. My heart and my conscience were touched—I needed to be reconciled to my siblings. But I argued with the Lord. I said, "Lord, they've been Christians longer than I, they've hurt me far more than I've hurt them." The Lord said, Be reconciled. I went to them as individuals for forgiveness, for very specific things I had done to hurt and offend them, instances where I'd gossiped about them. They gave me their forgiveness. You know, the consequences of forgiveness are out of all proportion to the effort it takes to seek it. It's wonderful.

Recently, I wrote a book. And in the process of writing it, I learned many things about myself, things that others told me. Shelby, for example, shared with me that she made a commitment to God when we were courting that she would never criticize me. You can't imagine what that meant to this insecure person, although that's not always the most healthy thing in the world, because she needed to share some things with me. But God knew that I needed a wife who was supportive in that special way. Another piece in place.

In 1971 we were back on the field, in Papua New Guinea, and our friend began talking about forgiveness in a way we hadn't heard before, using terms like the healing of the memories. That's not the taking away of a memory. We don't want that. But it's healing the hurt of those painful memories. And so we asked to be prayed for. Our missionary colleagues laid their hands on us and prayed. Well, my wife reminded me while I was writing the book that before I was prayed for, I had been picking at her for everything. She couldn't do anything right. She didn't feed the children right, she didn't dress right, she didn't look right, she didn't act right. I picked at her constantly. But after

God healed my memories, I changed. It was absolutely miraculous. I stopped picking at her, and I was a very different person.

Perhaps you're wondering, *Can God use imperfect, broken persons? Can God use me?* My parents went to China in 1921. They spent two years studying the Tibetan language. After that, they relocated to my birthplace, Hetzou, and they ministered there, faithfully preaching and teaching the Word of God. They did a lot of medical work and so forth. After four years in China, they had their first convert. He was a son of a chieftain, a very influential man in the whole region, and his life was transformed by the hope of Jesus and the gospel. The fear of demons and devils was gone and he talked about it. As he shared with others, people became interested and wanted more information about the Jesus way. Two weeks after he was converted, he was killed by his neighbors. They took his body and tied it up with rope. They stuffed stones in his mouth, and they tied the rope and his body behind a horse and dragged it through the streets of Hetzou, as a reminder to everyone of what would happen to them if they followed these foolish foreign Jesus ways.

The mission leaders suggested to my parents that they might want to move to a different location. But they didn't instruct them to move, and so, being called to that location, they stayed there for twenty-three years. At the end of that time, while there were many secret converts who came to Bible studies, preaching services and other activities, you could count the overt converts on one hand.

In 1961, while they were living in Ithaca, a letter arrived from India. It was from a Swedish Pentecostal missionary, who had reaped some of the ripe grain of Tibetan refugees that had migrated out of Tibet with the Dalai Lama. These Tibetans had become believers, and this Swedish missionary had gone to great lengths to find my parents. All he knew about them was my dad's name and some of the things that my father and mother had done for these Tibetans. A man whose leg bone my father had set had become a Christian. Another whose gonorrhea he had been instrumental in curing had become a Christian. A person he'd pulled a tooth for had become a Christian. A woman whose head had been split open had become a Christian. My dad had sewed her back up again and, miraculously, she had lived.

It was a long letter, and there was a long list of names of Tibetans to whom my parents had faithfully ministered for those twenty-three years.

In 1986, another friend was teaching in West China. He said that the church in Hetzou has a substantial number of Tibetans in it, and that the church around Hetzou has more than ten thousand believers. In spite of their brokenness, God used my parents. I had no idea God was using my parents. I wasn't even open to the possibility! And despite my brokenness, God has used me.

God's Love in You

Perhaps you're wondering, *How do I get started? Where can I get help?* Some time back, I started to have heart pains. I thought I was having a heart attack. I thought I might die. I got scared. God got my attention. I went to the InterVarsity leadership and told them, "God's got my attention. Shelby and I need to go to the desert and listen to him." They gave me their blessing and we went off.

Someone put into my hands a book that I commend to you. It's entitled *Twelve Steps—A Spiritual Journey,* written by Friends in Recovery. I want to share three principles from that book with you.

First, we have to acknowledge that we are powerless without God. Our life is unmanageable. Romans 7:18 says nothing good lives in our sinful nature.

Second, we have to believe that there is a power greater than ourselves that can restore us. This principle is based on Philippians 2:13: "for it is God who works in you to will and to act according to his good purpose."

And then, third, we must turn our will and lives over to God's care. Romans 12:1 says, "offer your bodies as living sacrifices."

Some of the broken pieces of my life are together. The glue that has repaired them has actually made each joint stronger than it was before it was broken. Jesus said, and I remind you, that his strength is made perfect in our weakness. A few pieces of my life are still not in place.

The pot that I glued back together looks beautiful, but it doesn't hold water. I wasn't as skillful as the tinker men of China. But it's still a wonderful reminder that God is concerned about my life—even those parts that are not quite in place. Fortunately, he's not finished with me.

God wants to be the tinker man of your life. He can put together your broken life. Perhaps you've got your own area of brokenness. God may be touching an area of your life right now—perhaps some deep hurt or painful memory, a conflict with your parents, a sibling, coworker, roommate or spouse, perhaps an abuse that you've experienced, perhaps a person you need to forgive. Let God minister to you right now. Let God bring wholeness to your life, in whatever area, just as he has done and continues to do in my life. There is hope for your hurts.

As we reflect upon Calvary and the pain of the world, we have the privilege of inviting God to meet us in our personal pain. This is the wonderful nature of God's love. We are not asked to address the ills of society at the expense of our own well-being. God's love flows both into our lives and through our lives. There is a sense in which we can bring the love of Christ to the world only to the degree to which we have experienced that love ourselves. We cannot lead others to something outside our own journey.

When Christ calls us to take his love into all the world, he is also asking us to place all our pain at his feet—to allow him the work of healing our souls. At times we are tempted to accept a view of God that is less than biblical, a view that says we have to *earn* God's acceptance through our deeds of sacrifice . . . and perhaps in time we can expect God to address our own pain. Not so! We are deeply loved. "I have loved you with an everlasting love;" says the Lord—"I have drawn you with loving-kindness" (Jer 31:3).

In fact, we cannot be faithful to the gospel if we attempt to "serve" the world without deeply falling in love with God, without allowing God to meet us at our place of longing. When we ask others to put their trust in the loving, trustworthy person of Jesus Christ, we are asking them to take a leap of faith. We need to lead them by our own example of faith.

This can be a risky affair, to be sure, especially if we carry deep hurts from other relationships. God is patient with us and will not push us further than our hearts and faith can manage. But we must launch out on this journey of love and faith. We must go through the difficult work of exposing our raw need and aspirations to the tender arms of Christ. There is no other pathway to love. And there is no more rewarding pathway in life. Jesus says, "Come to me, all you who are weary and burdened, and I will give you rest" (Mt 11:28). And again, "Take my yoke upon you . . . and you will find rest for your souls" (Mt 11:29).

Yes, it's an altar call for Christians! And if we had any idea of the wonderful gift waiting for us at the end of the aisle, we would throw off all the chains that keep us from trusting Jesus' love and we'd shout "Hallelujah!" as we sprinted forward into his arms.

Society's Pain

God's love for the world is perfect in the sense that he feels society's pain precisely. Perhaps that is part of what separates us from God: we are able to shut out the pain of society—it does not always touch our hearts. But not so with God. This is good news for the world. It is the intense pain of the world that drove Jesus to the cross and that continues to move him like a restless lover over the face of the earth, wooing all sorts of people in every sort of place.

God's love is also complete. By that we mean there is no pain in society that falls below the concern of God's heart, no pain that is insignificant or unimportant to our Lord. If you tabulate all the cries of the world—the cry of the hungry, the oppressed, the prisoner, the orphan, the widow, the naked, the mournful, the outcast, the sick, the depressed, the unforgiven, the abused, the lonely, the abandoned—you have described the tears of God.

How great is the love of God? Listen to the cries.

This is exceptionally good news. Some have wrongfully attributed to God a truncated love—an impoverished love that cares only about men and women's *souls*. This woefully incomplete depiction of God has in fact been an excuse for some to live above the needs of society, to preach a gospel that separates us from our bodies. About this Scripture warns us: "Dear children, let us not love with words or tongue but with actions and in truth" (1 Jn 3:18). And the picture given of the end times, where Jesus warns us not to ignore the hungry, thirsty, naked, prisoner—at the expense of our eternal well-being—is ample indication of his revulsion over a truncated love.

There is no tension between loving people's souls and feeding their hungry stomachs. We are called into a wonderful ministry of reconciliation—a ministry that brings all of life under the love of Jesus. That includes physical needs, emotional needs, spiritual needs, societal needs—all of the painful results of the Fall which need God's restorative touch through us. It's a ministry that refuses to allow the impact of the Fall to be the final statement of life. There is no more wonderful life that we can live.

We are invited to join Christ and the whole body of Christ in listening to the pain of society—in all its diverse and tormenting expressions—and saying, *Yes, Lord, send me.* Society couldn't ask for a better fix.

Romancing the Globe

Jesus told his disciples, as recorded in Mark 12:29-31, that all of the requirements of the law are fulfilled in two great commands:

> Love the Lord your God with all your heart and with all your soul and with all your mind and with all your strength. . . . Love your neighbor as yourself.

There is nothing to add to these two requirements. They fully describe the Christian life. When we accept the forgiving love of Jesus into every area of our lives, we are called to return that love to God. We are called to put into God's hands every part of who we are: our intellect, our emotions, our aspirations, our bodies, our personalities. Notice that God does not say, "*Obey* me with your heart, soul, mind and strength." He certainly has the right to ask that of us, but God is by nature love, and we are called to become like him, living through a redeemed self that has been transformed by his love. Lordship, when described more precisely, is really loveship. It is a relationship where persons devote themselves to one another in complete, unrestrained love. Jesus has already done that for us, and he is inviting us to return the love to him. It's the perfect romance story and we all have the option of writing some of the lines.

But it is a costly love. It extends to every level of human pain. And we are called not only to receive God's love personally, not only to turn all of our affections back to him, but to turn our love to our neighbors. We are called into the worldwide focus of God's love. Indeed, we are partners in the great adventure of romancing the globe.

It is as though we acquire the restless heart of God. The more we are transformed into his image, the less we are able to shut out the pain of society, the less we are able to live a life that ignores the human dilemma. The question that faces us now is: Will we join in God's untiring effort to bring all of society into his love? Will we become people who are known as those who were able to absorb the pain of the globe, when we had the choice to live for ourselves? The world does not understand this kind of love, to be sure, but it desperately longs to experience it.

We have no higher calling than to live inside the pain of the world. Some would teach that we should retreat from those parts of society that are marked by violence, poverty, hardship and desperation. Such people have not been captured by the romance, they haven't tasted of the love of Jesus. Their lives, in fact, are impoverished, as they lack the call of the wild upon their imaginations. Some of them, unfortunately, are religious leaders. Jesus met them in his day, those naysayers who accused him of hanging around the prostitutes, tax collectors, swindlers and beggars. Those accusations were meant to hurt his reputation. Jesus' response was, "Precisely! You got it. This is exactly what I am about."

The call to romance the globe is the call to live inside the pain of this world, to seek out the places of hopelessness, despair, destruction and evil and plant ourselves in the center of it. There, by the grace of God's love at work in us, we become the hands, feet and arms of Jesus. We wrap ourselves about the human dilemma and we become the tenderness, righteousness, mercy and justice of our Lover.

We are not of those who shrink back, who avoid pain, who insulate themselves from the hardships of this life. On the contrary, we "take up our cross," in the fashion of Jesus, and we willingly die outside the city gate on a garbage dump, taking on the despair and shame of all the world. And we do this because we ourselves have been romanced! We have found a love that is worth the price of everything we own and are. And we have been set loose to join in the global revolution of love.

The apostle Paul was captured by this great love. He heard the call of the wild and he lived the impossible life of loving others. He prays this prayer for us:

I pray that out of his glorious riches he may strengthen you with power through his Spirit in your inner being, so that Christ may dwell in your hearts through faith.

And I pray that you, being rooted and established in love, may have power, together with all the saints, to grasp how wide and long and high and deep is the love of Christ, and to know this love that surpasses knowledge—that you may be filled to the measure of all the fullness of God.

Now to him who is able to do immeasurably more than all we ask or imagine, according to his power that is at work within us, to him be glory in the church and in Christ Jesus throughout all generations, for ever and ever! Amen. (Eph 3:16-21)

Go ahead: Howl at the moon, romance the globe.

3
Blessed
to Be
a Blessing

You've heard about the Dead Sea: it has no outlet. Whatever comes in, it retains. It constantly receives, never giving away. Over time the sun and the wind suck the moisture from its surface, leaving behind deposits of salt. Slowly, at an imperceptible pace, the Dead Sea became poisonous to life, too concentrated in salts. And thus its name. If the Dead Sea had an outlet where water flowed freely downstream, poisonous deposits would not have built up. As it is, the Dead Sea is useless to provide life for anything. It's a twenty-minute bus stop for tourists.

The story of the Dead Sea is a parable of what happens to us if we keep our blessings to ourselves, and it's an important parable for Christians who desire to live a robust, healthy life.

Abraham and Sarah's Story: Faith
When God first fashioned the nation of Israel, he began with a family. Abraham and Sarah were called by God to leave their familiar setting and to

go far away "to the land I will show you"(Gen 12:1). They were being asked
to depart on a journey of faith for the purposes of God. In Genesis we read
about that purpose.

God desired to bless all the nations of the earth. The globe was crippled
with the consequences of the Fall, and God had determined to woo the world
back to himself by forming a nation that would become the community of
God. These people would serve to point others to God by the way they lived
their lives and demonstrated the character of Yahweh. God would bless them
in order for them to be a blessing:

> The LORD had said to Abram [later to become Abraham], "Leave your
> country, your people and your father's household and go to the land I will
> show you.
>
> "I will make you into a great nation and I will bless you;
>
> I will make your name great, and you will be a blessing.
>
> I will bless those who bless you, and whoever curses you I will curse;
>
> and all peoples on earth will be blessed through you." (Gen 12:1-3)

The life of Abraham and Sarah was not easy. They had to face unfriendly
people, famine and their own inability to have children. Since Sarah was
barren, they attempted to have children through a slave woman, and this only
caused animosity and pain. Abraham was not as strong as we would expect
the founding father of Israel to be: twice he allowed foreign leaders to take
his wife from him (pretending she was his sister) for fear they would kill him
to get her.

Their lives didn't exactly fit the normal pattern. Follow their story in the
pages of Genesis. When they are both very old, an angel visits them to remind
them of God's promise to make them into a great nation that will bless all
other nations. Abraham and Sarah are in disbelief, but God does not abandon
them. They are still willing to serve as God desires. God grants them a son,
Isaac. Then, before the child is old enough to have his own children, we see
this strange requirement of God placed on Abraham: "Take your son, your
only son, Isaac, whom you love, and . . . sacrifice him there as a burnt
offering" (Gen 22:2).

Abraham sets out on a three-day journey to fulfill this duty. What fills his mind and heart as he anticipates the sacrifice of his son *(please, Yahweh, find someone else to bless)?* But he persists. He gets to the point of tying up Isaac and raising the knife to slit his throat. At this moment Yahweh intervenes through an angel and provides a ram for the sacrifice. God is elated at Abraham's obedience and says, "I will surely bless you . . . and through your offspring all nations on earth will be blessed, because you have obeyed me" (Gen 22:17-18).

Abraham was willing to give up his most precious belonging to obey the word of God. Though difficult to understand, this test shows the faith in God held by the First Couple in the drama of Israel.

A Nation Is Born

In time we see Israel growing to become a mighty nation. They go from being the family of Abraham and Sarah to being a small clan, and then they grow to the point they are recognized as a small nation. The story is not exactly flattering. Jealousy, murder and lying make up the script of this nation that is to become God's instrument to bless all the nations. Abraham's grandson Jacob gives birth to twelve sons, and this is where jealousy finds its worst expression. Joseph is Jacob's favorite. The other brothers decide to sell him off into slavery, and he ends up in the courts of Pharaoh in Egypt.

A global famine strikes the world. Jacob sends his sons to Egypt to buy food, because the word is out that Pharaoh has a top assistant who has anticipated the global famine and has stored massive amounts of grain. This assistant is their brother Joseph. They meet, and a wonderful time of reconciliation follows, with the Pharaoh's invitation for the entire family to move to Egypt.

Before long, Israel becomes so wealthy in their abundance of children, livestock and grain that the Pharaoh decides to enslave them. For four hundred years the nation of Israel experiences the silence of God. These years of recounting the promise that they would be greatly blessed in order to bless others—while seeing no evidence of God's sending that blessing—must have required all their faith to believe.

In time God uses Moses to free Israel from Egypt, and they settle the

Promised Land after forty years of wandering through the desert. Israel has to organize itself into a great army to acquire the land of Canaan. Each battle becomes another symbol of God's intent as miraculous events accompany them on the battlefield.

As the years progress for this tiny nation, they decide they want a king, just like all the other nations. This distresses God, who would prefer to govern them directly. They insist, and God calls Saul to be their first king—warning them that taxes and military conscription will ensue! Saul is eventually replaced by David, the shepherd boy who exercised such great faith to kill a giant working for an enemy nation, the Philistines. It is David who takes Israel forward in its next great step as a nation devoted to Yahweh. Follow his story in 1 and 2 Samuel.

David's Story: Triumph and Defeat

David is the only person to whom the Bible refers as "a man after God's own heart." Not that his life was blameless—David went to the extent of murder to get Bathsheba as his wife (after an adulterous affair with her). Yet something about his heart captures the heart of God. The Psalms are the record of this man's struggles and desires to live right. Not only does he want to follow the ways of Yahweh in his own life, he wants Israel to bless the other nations. Somehow he is able to reach way back to days prior to Israel's captivity in Egypt and recall the desire of God to bless all the nations through Israel. David reflects this understanding in Psalm 67:

May God be gracious to us and bless us
    and make his face shine upon us,
that your ways may be known on earth,
    your salvation among all nations.
May the peoples praise you, O God;
    may all the peoples praise you.
May the nations be glad and sing for joy,
    for you rule the peoples justly
    and guide the nations of the earth.
May the peoples praise you, O God;

> may all the peoples praise you.
> Then the land will yield its harvest,
> and God, our God, will bless us.
> God will bless us,
> and all the ends of the earth will fear him.

David requested permission of God to build a temple as a center of worship. He genuinely desired a place that would be a testimony to the greatness of Yahweh. God not only complied, he also gave David the specific designs. The only limitation was that David himself would not be allowed to build it, because he loved war too much and had done so much killing.

God's desire to bless all the nations was made evident in the design of the temple. It was to be built to include a courtyard for all the nations. The Israelites would have to physically pass through that courtyard area in order to reach their own place of worship. The message was clear enough: you cannot worship Yahweh without the understanding that God is a global God. This courtyard was also to be a place where the orphan, widow and otherwise needy person could assemble—not for any particular time of worship, but just to receive the affirmation of God.

Israel was regularly told through the words of the prophets that God wanted them to be a nation that received and helped the strangers, aliens and needy. At no point in their history were they relieved of the notion that they were to be a blessing to others. Unfortunately, Israel chose to go against the designs of God. What was once a powerful nation that demanded the respect of all surrounding nations became a weak, embattled one, vulnerable to the attacks of neighboring countries. God regularly warned Israel of their impending doom. It did not have to occur, God told them through the prophets, but it would happen if they forsook the commands of the Lord.

Israel did not go God's way. In fact, besides forsaking the call to become a blessing to all nations, Israel got tired of Yahweh and took on the gods of other nations. They began to worship idols, celebrate pagan feasts and order their lives around the worship of the stars. God labels Israel a whore. And after several attempts to woo them back to his original intentions for them, he abandons them to captivity in Babylon. Nothing more is said;

there are several hundreds of years of silence.

Then, as with the time in Egypt, God makes himself known to Israel again. This time, instead of Moses the conquering freedom fighter who takes them out of captivity, Jesus comes in the form of a baby, becomes an itinerant rabbi whose teachings are strange, and is eventually killed by the rulers of the occupying forces. Not many Jews had the eyes of faith, this time, to recognize their Savior.

Jesus and the New Israel

The coming of Christ was predicted in the Old Testament in several different forms. Earlier we looked at one of the passages (Is 61) where Jesus is announced as the one who would bring true healing to all people in need. Jesus launched his public ministry on earth by going to a meeting in a synagogue and reading that passage—adding, "Today this scripture is fulfilled in your hearing." We read this in Luke 4:16-30. There is no doubt in the synagogue leaders' minds that Jesus is claiming to be the one foretold by Isaiah. They are so infuriated with his suggestion that they try to throw him down a cliff, but somehow Jesus evades them by just walking through the crowd.

It is at this point that the story of God's desire to bless all the nations becomes a confrontation with the nation he originally called to this work. As Jesus goes through towns and villages, healing diseases, teaching about ways to please God, forgiving sins and feeding the hungry, the Jewish leaders become desperate to get rid of him. Perhaps they really believe he is a threat to God's long-term promise to bless them, or perhaps they have grown hard in their hearts and prefer to ignore God. We do not really know. But we do get a glimpse of the escalating war, and Jesus spares no words in chastising them for their disobedience to his original purposes.

We must not miss the pain that goes with this drama. These are the exact people whom God set aside with special favor. He loved them "with an everlasting love" (Jer 31:3). He "conceived them in love." And as we hear later in the New Testament, he weeps over Jerusalem: "O Jerusalem, Jerusalem . . . how often I have longed to gather your children together as a hen gathers her chicks under her wings" (Mt 23:37). Jerusalem was to be the city of Zion, God's holy hill. Every valley would be raised and every mountain lowered to make a straight path to this great city of salvation. And now the Israelites have become a stiff-necked people who will not allow other nations to experience the blessing of Yahweh.

As Jesus pursues the path that will eventually take him to Calvary, he is doing it with all the sorrow of a parent who has experienced the loss of a child and a lover who has experienced the loss of a beloved. This is no doctrinal pursuit, this road to Calvary. This is the drama of love in its most painful and glorious expression.

Shortly before his final tour of Jerusalem where he is arrested by the Roman soldiers (at the request of the Jewish leaders), Jesus clears the temple. The statement of this act must not be missed. What was reserved as the courtyard for all the nations (per the instructions given to king David) had become a plaza for the Jewish leaders to make money off of people coming to make sacrifices to Yahweh. Commerce, racism and selfish gain had supplanted the intention of God. So Jesus makes a whip and clears out the money changers. While doing it he accuses them of taking the "house of prayer for all nations"—Jesus is quoting from Isaiah 56:7 here—and turning it into a "den of robbers" (Mk 11:17). The Pharisees are absolutely outraged by his insolence and they plot his death.

The message of Jesus to the Jewish leaders goes beyond merely "You didn't fulfill your duty to be a blessing to all nations." There is no neutral ground with God if you have experienced the blessing of his hand. No, indeed, the Israelites had become *thieves.* They were literally stealing the good news from the nations, as far as God was concerned. They were being judged on much harsher grounds than apathy.

Jesus is arrested, taken to trial and crucified. As he completes his final work of grace he cries out the words, "It is finished!" At that moment the curtain in the temple, that blocks the way to the Holy of Holies, is torn in two from top to bottom. The separation from the former system is complete. No longer will this selfish nation serve as the conduit for God's blessing to other nations. They have forfeited that right. Now, it will be the broken body of

Christ that will serve as the curtain to the Holy of Holies. Jesus will serve as the advocate between the people and the Father. And *everyone* will have access to the holy place! In fact, according to the New Testament authors, the true children of Abraham and Sarah now are those who, like this First Couple, place their faith in God. Those who follow Jesus have become the new Israel. And our kingdom is not of this world.

You can imagine the smug conversations of the Jewish leaders as reports relayed back to the temple from Golgotha gave the progress of the madman messiah hanging on the cross. Then all of a sudden the curtain rips in two and the sky goes dark and a terrible storm takes over the city for hours. Clearly, Yahweh had spoken. The question for them becomes: Will you join the new Israel, or will you continue to live the selfish life of retaining blessings for yourself? We know that, unfortunately, too many of them chose the latter.

The New Kingdom Grows

The disciples caught the vision of spreading the good news. The early days of the church are marked with incredible stories of courage, faith, sacrifice and witness. These men and women knew they were a part of the new kingdom, and they knew that God intended this gospel of grace and love to spread over all the earth.

The day of Pentecost was a dazzling kickoff for this new global effort. The Holy Spirit was there and gave dramatic and miraculous signs.

One morning the disciples are out preaching about the risen Christ who has also ascended into heaven. All of a sudden they receive the ability to preach in different languages—thirteen in all, by the account of the New Testament witness who wrote the story down. In Jerusalem, which served as a marketplace crossroads of several nations, all those different languages were represented. Merchants and traders heard the good news in their own languages and responded (we are told that on that day alone, several thousand joined the new kingdom). And then these men and women took the gospel back to their own countries.

We have the account, too, of Philip being led into the desert to meet a traveling Ethiopian who is trying to understand the writings of the prophet

Isaiah. Philip explains to him how Jesus has become the fulfillment of those prophecies, and right there the fellow is baptized. He returns to Ethiopia and may very well have played a leading role in that nation's great heritage of the gospel.

Saul, one of the chief persecutors of Christians, is blinded as Jesus speaks to him from heaven through a light flashing around him. Saul is dramatically converted and becomes Paul, the greatest missionary of all time.

Not all of the stories are miraculous. In fact, the majority of the accounts of people working to extend the kingdom in those New Testament days are the stories of ordinary men and women who refused to retain the blessing for themselves. And they spread the good news at tremendous cost to themselves. The ruling emperor of Rome was persecuting Christians for their faith. If they did not proclaim Caesar as Lord, they were thrown to the lions, burned as living torches at night and tortured by means so cruel that they have not been "improved" upon since. Historians write with amazement at how these Christians refused to bow the knee to Caesar. They had met their new King, and they were going to bring as many as they could along with them.

The disciples went throughout the entire known world at the time, with the apostle Thomas going as far as India. We read from historical accounts that all but one of the apostles were probably killed for their faith—in the act of spreading the blessing to others in defiance of all attempts to stop them. Peter was supposedly hung upside down on a cross in mockery of Jesus' crucifixion. Obviously these missionaries of the gospel were clear in their message. They caught the vision that God had introduced to Abraham, and they faithfully became a channel of the good news for other.

The book of Revelation, as mentioned earlier, is a wonderful promise to the church that God will prevail in his desire to bring *all the nations* under his blessing. The rich spiritual heritage we enjoy will see its completion when Christ returns. One day there will be a great banquet and at the table will be members of all tribes, tongues and nations.

Those who experienced the great trial of presenting the good news of Jesus in the face of adversity will not go unnoticed by the King at the end of time. They will be dressed in white robes in heaven. This will be a symbol that the blood of persecution has been washed from them.

They are before the throne of God
and serve him day and night in his temple;
and he who sits on the throne will spread his tent over them.

Never again will they hunger;
never again will they thirst.

The sun will not beat upon them,
nor any scorching heat.

For the Lamb at the center of the throne will be their shepherd;
he will lead them to springs of living water.

And God will wipe away every tear from their eyes. (Rev 7:15-17)

We should not miss the contrast this moving account provides to the final encounter Jesus had with the Jewish leaders before his death. They mocked him and called insults up to him as he hung on the cross. They missed the point of being a blessing to others—and so, at the end, they missed the welcome reception of Jesus. But not so for those martyrs of the faith who have gone before us in the wonderful work of spreading the blessing to the ends of the earth.

Our Bodies—the New Temple

We are left with some personal questions as we reflect on the idea of "blessed to be a blessing." Clearly, we must accept that those who are called into fellowship with Christ carry the obligation of extending that blessing to others. We never are given the blessing as private property. Oh, yes, we do experience all the personal blessings that go with encountering Christ, but this blessing is not owned by us. The blessing is a public trust. It is as though Christ makes us trustees of the blessing. He puts it into our care until he returns at the end of time. We are faced with the question: Will he find us to be faithful trustees of his kingdom—or will he return to find us similar to the Jewish leaders who retained the blessings of Yahweh for themselves? It's our decision.

In June of 1993, Victor Santana, a third-year student at Trinity Evangelical Divinity School, and Isaac Canales, an inner-city pastor from Los Angeles, made a trip to Havana, Cuba, to arrange an InterVarsity Global Project for the summer of 1994. Victor is the designated director. As a Dominican American whose first language is Spanish and who has the experience of three Global Projects in the former USSR, he is ideally suited to lead this strategic program. Victor went on his first Global Project in 1990, to Kiev. During his project the group was joined by six college presidents and representatives of three relief and developmental agencies to host a special relief and development symposium. At the close of the symposium, the host insisted that a worship service be held, led by the InterVarsity students. Victor gave a brief but powerful message, telling how Jesus had changed his own life and challenging the audience to consider the claims of Christ. The previous evening, Victor had shared at the large-group worship meeting, along with several of the Spanish-speaking Ukrainian students who had become Christians that summer as a result of his witness.

During the following summer, Victor served on the staff team of the Kiev Global Project at the Kiev State Pedagogical Institute of Foreign Languages. There were students on that project from several countries in the former USSR. Victor's leadership contributed significantly to the productivity of the summer.

During the summer of 1992, Victor directed the project in Kiev. Several Ukrainian students became Christians that summer, and all the other Ukrainians moved along that continuum from unbelief to belief. Victor and his team of staff and students continue the vital relationships they developed during the summer projects.

On his recent trip to Havana, when asked about his future, Victor said, with a twinkle in his eye, "I'm not absolutely certain, but I have a strong inclination toward serving the Lord in world missions."

One of the members of the Moscow Global Project in 1991 was a student from Central Asia by the name of Ibrahim. Ibrahim had not been told by his hosts that he was coming to spend the summer with a group of Christians. And he was very upset by this fact. He was matched with Don, who had been praying for months and preparing himself to spend the summer with a Russian roommate. He too was disappointed. Ibrahim, being a religious Muslim, brought everything around him to a halt as he faithfully prayed five times a day to Allah. The InterVarsity students patiently waited during each of these prayer times.

Before long, friendships began. By the end of the summer, Ibrahim and the InterVarsity students were very close friends, especially Ibrahim and Don. At the farewell celebration, Ibrahim asked the director, Chuck Ellis, if he could pray to Allah for his blessing on the group. Chuck welcomed him to do this. Before Don and Ibrahim parted, Don challenged him: "Ibrahim, I will study your religious book if you will study mine. Let's commit ourselves to study one another's religious books until one of us converts."

In the course of the next year, Don studied the Koran, and Ibrahim studied the New Testament, all alone in his city and without any help from other Christians. Don and he carried on a vigorous correspondence; other members of the group wrote him as well.

In March of the next year, Ibrahim laid down his commitment to Islam. He called Moscow to ask our hosts if the group would be returning and if he could return to Moscow as a member of the host group.

Ibrahim came back with many tough questions about Christianity. Some of them were not perfectly answered. However, by the end of the summer Ibrahim had made a commitment to Christ. He requested that InterVarsity take a Global Project to the university where he had begun working as an instructor of English. In February of the following year, a team visited his university, exploring the possibility of a Global Project. They were welcomed by the authorities there. During the summer of 1993, six more Central Asian students became believers.

One of the steps that InterVarsity is taking to help in this situation is to place a team year-round in this city. Don will be leading this team and will be joined by some others that went for the summer. These student workers will spend time learning the Kahzakh language while taking steps to help Ibrahim and the students organize a Christian fellowship there.

God's Temple in Today's World

Let's return to the image of the temple. This was the center of the life for the people of Israel. Their primary religious expressions took place in this building. The Holy of Holies, which could be accessed only by the high priest, held the ark of the covenant. This box, carried on poles, represented the holy agreement, the covenant, between the Israelites and God: *I will be your God if you will be my people. I will bless you so that you can become a blessing to all the nations.* As we have learned, Israel failed to keep the covenant, failed to become a conduit of God's blessing to all the world.

There is no central temple today for the new Israel, for the spiritual children of Abraham and Sarah, for those who live by faith in Jesus Christ. There is no physical location that draws us all together. Indeed, as we heard earlier, God's new kingdom is not of this world. But our calling does not change. No, we are not of this world, but we are to remain in it and become a channel of God's blessing to all the world in its diverse makeup and diverse pain.

The Bible says that we are now the temple of the Holy Spirit (1 Cor 6:19). We do not belong to ourselves. God has built a new temple. It is each one of us who has received the blessing.

The question we face then, is, how will God find our temple when he returns? Will we have been faithful to his desire to make a place for all the nations, aliens, and needy people? Will the courtyard of our inner self be a place preoccupied with notions of personal gain, or will it be the busy intersection of a life of love for people who live outside the blessing? Will it serve as a place of tenderness, mercy, forgiveness and justice for the world around us?

We have been given the wonderful privilege of blessing others. It truly is an honor. Hundreds of thousands have been captured by this vision of life; they can be found in distant lands and at home, planting churches where the gospel is not known, feeding the hungry, caring for prisoners, working on behalf of the oppressed, translating the Bible, providing clean water for impoverished societies, teaching people to read, parenting orphans and providing medical care. These people are channels of the love of Jesus, and they are inviting others to be channels with them. Their lives are bright, welcome temples that sit on hills across the globe. They cannot be hid. They cannot be deterred. And the world thanks God for them.

4
Generation X

Each generation writes its own story, determines its own destiny. It's a choice. The question facing Generation X is, Will it write a story of love? Will it set a course of courage, compassion and hope? Or will it leave behind a legacy of detachment and apathy?

Every generation faces two competing temptations. The first is to live a life measured by *comfort and personal gratification.* This lifestyle is marked by a calculated coldness—an ability to shut out the cries of society in order to pursue personal satisfaction. The fundamental deception that underlies this lifestyle is the idea that personal comfort is the highest good. People are convinced they will be "happier" if they can line up the ideal job, live in the ideal neighborhood, marry the ideal person, acquire the ideal kinds of toys and build up a substantial retirement. This goal looks a little bit like Disneyland. It's not real, but it is as large as life and all-consuming.

The personal cost is devastating. People who run this course are impoverished in their souls. They have exchanged the substance of their personhood (as God created them) for a counterfeit one. They are not living out the core of their identity. Rather, they have chosen to mimic a fairy tale.

We cannot ignore the needs of our souls. As we pursue our personal comfort at the expense of what is real, we become malnourished. We lose our ability to judge between value and vapor. And our ears eventually stop hearing the sounds of human pain. We don't know how confused we are. We believe we are living a life of substance, but all the while the real life is being drained from us.

The Bible warns of this process. First, we conceive an idea in our mind, then we give way to the pursuit of it, and in time this pursuit leads to our death.

There is plenty of razzle-dazzle to support this kind of life. Society rewards the people with the largest toys, the greatest power, the most money. The struts that hold us up are the approval of those who have chosen the same course, or those who wish they could join us—we gain their admiration. We stand tall and strong because of temporary struts, not because of internal personal substance. But then adversity removes our supports and we are devastated. We have no one to blame but ourselves.

In the end, those of us who have chosen this course of cold detachment are pathetic. We become bland, stale, lukewarm. We are desperately in need of being saved. Tragically, Christians are too often seduced by this hollow vision of life. As the Laodicean Christians of the early church did, we need to hear Jesus' words:

> I know your deeds, that you are neither cold nor hot. I wish you were either one or the other! So, because you are lukewarm—neither hot nor cold—I am about to spit you out of my mouth. You say, "I am rich; I have acquired wealth and do not need a thing." But you do not realize that you are wretched, pitiful, poor, blind and naked. I counsel you to buy from me gold refined in the fire, so you can become rich; and white clothes to wear, so you can cover your shameful nakedness; and salve to put on your eyes, so you can see.
>
> Those whom I love I rebuke and discipline. So be earnest, and repent. Here I am! I stand at the door and knock. If anyone hears my voice and opens the door, I will come in and eat with him, and he with me. (Rev 3:15-20)

We can hear God's contempt here. But we shouldn't miss the heart of these words—God is asking for the privilege of coming into our lives and enjoying fellowship with us! The pursuit of personal gratification as our highest good interrupts our communion with God and essentially leaves us banished from the Garden—that place of daily intimacy with our Father.

If we face this temptation of personal gratification as our highest good, we also face the competing temptation *to be great, to be significant.* Society elevates certain people above us and leaves us with the sense that we are somehow less than they. Movie stars, singers, athletes, corporate leaders and politicians, to name a few, are the "beautiful people." We wish that we could somehow attain their level.

The fundamental deception that underlies this temptation is the notion that we draw our significance through the approval of others. And so we spend massive amounts of energy and creativity working toward the goal of being well spoken of by others.

The ads tell us that certain purchases will bring us a little closer to the status of famous people. We are tempted to buy certain jeans, cars, shampoos, perfumes, shoes, ice creams and beverages simply because they'll put us in the circle of celebrity habits. We probably are not aware to what degree we follow this temptation. Take inventory of your recent purchases: how much have you bought into this deception?

And we regularly receive messages from our culture that only certain jobs are worthy of our human dignity. If we want to be noticed by others, if we want to gain their approval, we will commit our lives to an educational/vocational track that fits the cultural requirements.

This lifestyle is just as impoverished as that of being devoted to personal gratification. There is no substance to our activities. Everything we commit ourselves to is just vapor, the desperate attempt of a poor self-image to find approval. Our lives are measured by others' opinions of us.

We cannot be free of this deception unless we ground ourselves in the notion of God's deep love for us. Our worth is measured by the fact that we are personally known by God, drawn to him by his everlasting love. We cannot gain a higher status than this. No human being is able to confer this level of significance upon us.

There is yet another level of temptation we face in this struggle to be significant. Christians, in particular, can be tempted to be *great doers of good*—to be known for their level of activism. It's the Mother Teresa syndrome. And by pursuing this role we may be looking for the approval of the Christian community in particular, versus society in general.

In Acts 5:1-11 we get a glimpse of this temptation through the apostle Peter's encounter with Ananias and Sapphira. The two of them sell a piece of property and decide to give the proceeds from the sale to the work of the church. When Ananias gives the money to Peter, he decides to retain some of it for personal use. No problem—except that he tells Peter *all* of the money from the sale is being given to the church as a gift.

Ananias so badly wants the approval of his Christian peers that he lies about the size of his donation. He can imagine the conversations about him: "Did you hear about Ananias? He is so generous!" And perhaps he is anticipating an appointment to some leadership post because of his obvious commitment to the work of Christ.

God gives the apostle Peter insight to Ananias's deception and, in one of the more bizarre New Testament accounts, Ananias drops dead on the spot. And as if it were the natural thing to do, several church members cart him off and bury him. Three hours later Sapphira shows up at church. She has not learned that her husband is dead and buried (a strange circumstance, to be sure!). Peter asks her about the donation. She too lies about the percentages. Peter condemns her, and within minutes the same men who buried her husband are carrying her body off to the graveyard.

We must ask why God made sure this event was included in the New Testament record. We do know from other passages that God abhors deception. But the misdeeds of Ananias and Sapphira go further than deception. We are left to wonder if perhaps these two had already died in their souls. Had they so thoroughly pursued the approval of the Christian community that they were now simply images of an idea, a reflection of people's opinions? Indeed, we are led to believe that Ananias and Sapphira had become so hardened by their own delusions of grandeur that they were willing to lie to God. Why, otherwise, would God act so harshly toward them for one instance of deception?

Clearly, it is dangerous to our souls for us to seek the approval of others. And as with the pursuit of comfort, we are supported by false struts. Our self-image is connected to our deeds, and a change in our circumstances can bring all of that crashing down. We are devastated—not because life has dealt us harsh blows, but because the truth about us has been revealed. We cannot bear to be exposed to the public; much worse, we cannot accept an honest description of who we have become by our own choices.

It is a pity that Ananias and Sapphira missed this truth: God does not look at the external nature of our deeds—God looks on the heart. And because only God can see the heart, only God has the capability of "rating" our service. Jesus took his disciples to the synagogue and showed them the contrast of giving externally and internally. Wealthy men brought bags of gold to the temple and in front of everyone poured their coins into the coffers. Truly an impressive display of generosity. Next, a poor widow ascended the synagogue steps and dropped two little coins in the coffer. Jesus told the disciples that she "gave more" than the others because she gave all she had.

We are in good hands with God. There is nothing we can do to earn his approval. His love for us is perfect and complete. We cannot increase his love for us by doing more good deeds, we cannot "up" our significance in the eyes of the one who conceived us in love and who constantly pursues us. Our significance before God is an established fact. The only work we have to do in this regard is the hard work of undoing the deception we have acquired over time—the lie that says we have to earn the Lover's approval.

The source of our doing good deeds in society draws from a well much deeper than our need to be significant. As we fall in love with Christ and are transformed into his image, we actually become transformed into loving people. Our very substance as people changes, and we now live our life out of this new substance. Our service to the world is no longer a function of our own personal needs, but a function of the fact that we have become a new creation. Sure, the commands to be obedient, to fulfill our duties to society and to make disciples of all nations are useful to motivate us into service, but our main motivation is the transformation brought about in us by the loving work of Christ.

And there is no deed of love too small to be significant. We learn this from the parable of the mustard seed. Jesus tells his disciples that serving the purposes of the kingdom has ramifications that go far beyond the specific act of service itself. The little that we do spreads its impact much farther than we would ever have presumed. Jesus told his disciples to imagine a mustard seed, which normally grows to a small flower, instead growing into a tree so large that birds build nests in it. Everyone listening to Christ knew that was impossible. And yet, said Jesus, that is how it goes with our deeds for the kingdom. There are no insignificant persons in God's kingdom; neither are there any insignificant deeds.

The Legacy of Generation X

We return then to the question of what story this generation will write in history. No generation is exempt from the temptation to pursue the false and pathetic road of personal gratification and significance. No generation is above the pull of cold-hearted detachment for the sake of comfort. No generation can escape the seduction of apathy for the rewards of personal gain.

Each generation has to find the contemporary path that transcends these vacuous pursuits. The moment for Generation X is here. Will you choose to write a story marked by courage, love and vision? Will you discover that the power of love is much stronger than the power of death? No other generation has the opportunity to respond to the unique challenges of today. No other generation will be given the task of defining what shape the gospel must take to address the pain of contemporary society. That privilege and responsibility belongs to this generation alone.

As Christians make their mark on each generation, they do it through the art of listening and feeling. They become expert in the ability to hear the cries of society, to feel precisely the pain, aspirations and longings of the people around them. They ensure that their lives are not marked by isolation and detachment from the human dilemma. Rather, they regularly look for means to fine-tune their listening and feeling skills. They look for opportunities to draw near to pain, and then they ask God for the grace to be a channel of love in that context. They add to these skills an astute understanding of the Word. Scripture becomes their guide to responding to the pain. In its pages they find the direction, encouragement and knowledge necessary to be a people of compassion—and the will to not grow weary in doing good.

What are the unique opportunities facing Generation X? What is the nature of our contemporary global society—the context for God's people to act? Below we have listed some of the key ways in which today's world waits for the loving involvement of Christians. There are more, to be sure, and each generation rewrites the list as it lives in the center of the human circumstance.

The Growth of Islam

Today there are as many as one billion people who are Muslim. They live under a tight system of belief that holds absolute submission to Allah as the pattern for all life—public and private. Entire governments operate from the pages of the holy book, the Koran, without the assistance of a national constitution. Daily routines of cleanliness, education, family life and vocation are guided by the principles of the Koran, making Islam the world's most integrated system of belief. And it is a closed system of belief. Islam is highly suspicious of any other religion; in most societies where Islam dominates, freedom of expression regarding other religions outside Islam is severely restricted.

Islam is the fastest-growing religion in the world today. It has dominated the Middle East for centuries; the discovery of oil in that region in the past fifty years has provided Islam with a financial boost that is seen as the blessing of Allah. And with that blessing comes the mandate to spread the Islamic message. Massive missionary undertakings, supported by billions of dollars, have led to Islamic inroads throughout the Christianized West. What once seemed to be the safe haven of Judeo-Christian beliefs is now the land of opportunity for those who would please Allah with their missionary zeal. Entire neighborhoods, schools and city councils in parts of Europe and the United States are now dominated by Islam. The force of this movement is only just beginning. Islam is now the fastest-growing religion in the United

States (it has found fertile ground among African-Americans), and fully fourteen percent of immigrants to the United States are Muslim.

Members of Generation X face a formidable challenge. And it is ironic that the symbol *X* has taken new significance in the African-American community with the resurgent popularity of Malcolm X, the martyred advocate of the Nation of Islam—Islam's most radical expression in the United States. There is probably no more challenging front for the work of the kingdom in the world today than the call to bring the gospel to Islamic societies.

The history of contention between Muslims and Christians carries a much greater hostility and suspicion than witnessed in Northern Ireland between the Catholics and Protestants. Stories of Christians attempting to annihilate Muslims with the sword (during the infamous Crusades of nearly a thousand years ago) are still transmitted through folklore and school in Islamic communities. And as a further complication, the presence of Western vices abhorred by Islamic society—alcohol, sexual looseness, pornography and the like—only increases the gap between Islamic and "Christian" societies. To many Muslims, *West* and *Christian* are synonymous, and therefore Christianity is a tool of Satan. We cannot diminish the significance of these conflicting worldviews. Muslims believe they are on a genuine quest to make Allah great among the nations. They bring with them theological expertise (from the Koran) and a lifestyle of devotion that includes regular prayer and fasting.

Students are making a difference in the world of Islam. Listen to the letter of an InterVarsity staff member who recently led a team of students on a friendship and cultural exchange:

The students are forming relationships most missionaries only dream of. Families, scattered across this country, have taken us into their homes. Mari is staying with a wealthy oil family. They took her on vacation with them and she got to hear how they think and what they value. Walt is with a man whose mother just died, so the family is in mourning. That means the extended family gets together every evening and just talks and spends time together. Three others are with the "happening" crowd. They go to parties, dances and festivals. These Muslim students look like they just stepped out of *Vogue* magazine. It's fascinating for our students to learn what makes them tick, and vice versa. Two others have so endeared themselves to the family they're staying with that their host told me she wasn't going to be bringing them to the airport!

It's not all roses. Gerta is with a woman who failed this past year and will have to repeat her university classes. Both of her parents are dead. All this has made for a bitter person. She resents Gerta's faith in God. Pray for a breakthrough in friendship. Pray that somehow they will come to love one another. Ask the Lord for strength for Gerta.

Our party time Saturday with the students went very well. I "married" one of our couples again, to show our host students how an American wedding looks. We served food. Then we sang for them. Then they sang for us and danced some more. We sang songs about loving God, and they sang songs about love. People hung around for hours afterward.

We're using public transportation. We look so lost most of the time we're used to helpful folks telling us in their language what to do (like, "Get off the train, this is the end of the line"). We have lost count how many times we have exited too soon, or too late. The most comical is when we chase after a metro (like a trolley) and catch it, only to find it doesn't open its doors at that stop. (It always makes great theater for the watching crowd.)

Pray for the students, pray for the families we're living with, pray for our safe return. In the next days we'll be trying to arrange for next year's program. I think the program has tremendous potential here. The government and the university seem to like us, and there's a lot of mutual respect. Christians who sense a call to live among Muslims will benefit from several steps of preparation:

1. Learn the history of Muslim contributions to society. These are numerous, ranging from medicine to art to architecture to math to literature.

2. Become a student of both the Koran and the historical development of Islam.

3. Learn the contemporary issues that drive Islam globally. For example, seek to understand the feelings of the Islamic community regarding the

Bosnia/Herzegovina conflict, or the freedom movement (of Muslims) in the former Soviet Union.

4. Establish friendships with Muslims.

5. Link up with a short-term mission agency that can give you a quality crosscultural experience with Muslims for a summer or for several months. This could begin to open the door for long-term possibilities.

6. If you are a student, seek a year-long academic program in an Islamic society. If you are in the marketplace, be on the lookout for job opportunities or transfers that will take you into an Islamic society.

7. Begin to link up with organizations that connect professionals with secular job openings in Muslim societies. Through this process God may lead you into relationship with a particular organization with whom you may serve over the long haul.

Urban Poverty

Literally millions of people each year are migrating into the cities of the world in the hopes of finding employment and a better life. Poverty in their rural circumstances, military conflict, or just the promise of a pot of gold at the end of the rainbow may serve to motivate folks to pull up roots and relocate.

Unfortunately, cities are not able to absorb these migrants at such a rapid rate. Every year millions of people end up in a strange place, unemployed, without housing or education or medical attention or sanitation. They are highly vulnerable to unscrupulous people; most of them experience some form of victimization, ranging from robbery to rape to enslavement to murder. Disease and starvation are typical, and both crime and prostitution become necessary means of survival for many who only a few months earlier were harvesting corn in their own back yards.

The problem of urban poverty touches a fifth of the world's population. It's not a problem to be "solved." The numbers are too staggering, and the complex web of circumstances is beyond any simple solution. But this should not deter Christians from engaging the issues.

Christ never called the church to make a "clean sweep" of society's ills. We are called to live in the centers of pain and there, by the work of the Holy

Spirit in our lives, to offer the tenderness, hope and creativity these particular people so clearly require. Christians land on a specific piece of the world and ask God to work through them at that location. This is the essence of what it means to have an incarnational ministry. It follows the life of Jesus who left the splendor of heaven, set up shop in Nazareth and there built his outreach around real people in real circumstances. The Scriptures never give us a picture of Jesus at work in society without listing in detail the names of people he encountered and particular ailments (be they sin, sickness, relational challenges or whatever) that he was addressing.

Holly went on an urban summer mission project hosted by Mission Ebenezer Family Church, serving south-central Los Angeles. The services are a wonderful display of the family of God, with both Spanish and English services and lovely folk from a number of different ethnic and racial backgrounds.

The project arranged by the church took Holly into a south-central Los Angeles elementary school where most of the children were primarily Spanish-speaking. Most of them were immigrant children, and all of them seemed to have a story of tragedy that was very close to them.

Holly had the privilege of spending the summer assisting Diane, a public school teacher who has a sense of call about service to the King in this situation. Diane makes house calls in parts of that city that most of us would be fearful of driving through.

One day the father of one of the students was beaten and shot in front of the little girl and three of her classmates. On a house call, Diane and Holly ended up on their knees along with the family, praying for the health of the father. The family was Christian and was trusting God for his blessing in this tragic situation. The man did recover.

Another day one of the children was acting up all day. That evening Diane and Holly made a house call. They discovered that the home was right next door to the spot where a drive-by shooting had occurred the night before. This child had seen the shooting.

Diane attended UC—Santa Barbara and was involved with InterVarsity there. She had become a Christian in her last few weeks of high school, as a result of being invited into a Christian home and experiencing a Christian family at meals. Her time with InterVarsity was a period of tremendous growth for her.

Midway through her college education, she wanted badly to go on a mission project, but couldn't afford to go overseas, so she made arrangements to seek employment in south-central Los Angeles. She got a job in a place where she had to speak Spanish. Her Spanish fluency accelerated. Commenting on her attendance at Urbana 90, she says, "I was propelled into the city with the love of the Lord Jesus." Diane doesn't know what the future holds for her, but she loves the children God puts in her classes. What a tremendous opportunity it was for Holly to experience the love of the Lord Jesus ministered through Diane, and to assist her in sharing that love through excellence in their teaching and in other ways in that needy community.

If you sense God calling you to urban ministry, here are a few steps you could take in that direction:

1. Research local ministries that work with the urban poor. See if there is a way you can volunteer each week in one of their programs.

2. Look through the "Urbana Options Guide" (available at Urbana or through InterVarsity). The guide will help you cross-check your interests with the needs of specific mission agencies. The matrix lets you narrow the choice down to regions of the world and work that relates to your major.

3. Become aware of the local issues that impinge upon the urban poor. Are there specific ways in which you could help address their concerns? These could range from legal counseling to literacy training to tutoring to job placement.

4. Look for opportunities to move into the inner city. Perhaps you could join a semester program if you are a student, or join a summer mission project. If you are in the work force, you may be able to find an urban assignment. Join a church that is either composed of urban poor or committed to ministry among them.

5. Read up on the city in general. Learn what makes it work and not work. Read literature regarding justice issues—these are often primary to people who are crunched in the machinery of inner cities.

6. Consider an academic program in community development. This approach to learning looks at the entire needs system of a local community and seeks means to address all the integrated needs simultaneously. A good Christian academic program will add the spiritual dimension.

7. Become aware of organizations that are looking for career staff in the inner city. Over time God may lead you to join up with one of these groups permanently.

Children with Desperate Needs

To grasp the suffering of children throughout the world, we need to picture them as they are in relation to adults—defenseless, weak, voiceless, unskilled and uninformed. When drought, famine, violence or war visits a region, children are the first to suffer and the last to receive help. And they have the least in personal resources—whether wealth or creative options—to care for themselves during times of calamity. Children are the first to die from disease (impure water is the leading cause of death for children globally). Children in the womb and in the first five years of their lives are especially vulnerable to the lack of certain nutrients. Their minds and bodies are still developing at critical stages. Malnutrition at this stage can lead to a lifetime of disability.

More than a hundred million children, aged six to fourteen, live on the streets. They have no parents, no houses, no jobs and no future. For them, survival means the art of robbery, con jobs and subsistence eating. Winter brings sickness and, for many, death. And they are the most vulnerable to the exploits of adults driven by evil intent. Every year hundreds of thousands of these street children are kidnapped off the streets for use in child prostitution, child pornography, snuff films and child labor. Several urban centers report the existence of a "sport" directed at street kids—drive-by shootings and death by fire.

Substance abuse becomes a way out of the pain for all too many of these children. Glue, rubbing alcohol, crack and gasoline become their friends and their ultimate demise. Gangs become the true families of these youth, and they quickly learn the art of violence. Human rights groups have documented the collusion of police with gang warfare because of the likelihood that these youth will "eliminate each other" through their fighting. Those who survive the streets live their adult years with severe brain and organ damage and are dependent on social programs until their death. Or they alternate between life on the streets and incarceration. There are very few accounts of happy endings to those who begin on the streets.

We learn from the Scriptures that God reserves a special place in his heart for "the least of these." When we mess with children we mess with God. And when we are a friend of children we are a friend of God.

Almost eighty-five percent of conversions to Christ take place between the ages of four and fourteen. Yet in spite of this fact, the vast majority of programs and resources, both in mission agencies and in the church, are aimed at adults. But, thankfully, there are ministries that focus on the world's children. Forms of outreach include urban centers where youth can receive hot meals, showers, a bed for the night and medical care. Some of these children are placed in homes where eventually they are adopted into loving families. Recreation centers offer an outlet for energy where the option of mischief is a strong magnet for kids with disposable time and no supervision. Literacy training, school education and skills development all become the building blocks for the chance of freedom from the streets.

Some organizations operate what are essentially rescue centers for youth—kids who, because of crises, enter the street life, unaware of the downward spiral they face. "Runaway" kids are quickly caught in prostitution and drug abuse. These rescue centers send out their staff to comb the streets, to literally rescue youth about to crash into the destructive life. Large billboards and flyers advertise toll-free numbers for kids to call when they realize they are vulnerable to forces outside their control.

A life of ministry to youth begins with some very simple steps:

1. Open your heart to the children in your neighborhood. Ask God to give you a special love for them and an insight on how you might reach out to them.

2. Connect with organizations that minister to youth. These could be as diverse as a sports organization, a youth-at-risk program, a big brother/big sister plan or a church.

3. Look for opportunities to gain crosscultural exposure to youth. Several organizations work with youth around the world and offer quality short-term mission programs in the summer.

4. Get involved in an urban setting. Most youth problems are lived out in this context. Become well acquainted with the phenomenon of gang life and juvenile delinquency.

5. Consider work in the area of public health. Poverty strikes children on many fronts. First-rate programs with an emphasis on Third World conditions are available in major North American universities.

People Very Unlikely to Hear the Good News

We spoke earlier of the Bible's promise that every tribe, tongue and nation will end up at the great banquet table of God in heaven at the end of time. The blood of Calvary will be effective to accomplish what Abraham was originally promised—that through his seed all the families on earth would be blessed.

But we have not yet reached the end of time. And perhaps as many as one-third of the world's people live in societies that are completely cut off from the good news of Jesus Christ. No churches or fellowships of believers are found in their cultures. They have no way of knowing about the forgiveness of sins and the promise of eternal life. The apostle Paul was thinking of them when he asked, "How can they hear about him unless someone tells them?" (Rom 10:14 LB). Unreached people groups are found primarily among Muslims, tribal people, Hindus and Buddhists. They are not in circumstances where they are likely to hear the good news.

Christians have to make concerted efforts to follow the model of Jesus' life where he left his home to live in another society. This fits the missionary calling at its heart, the same call given to Abraham and Sarah at the very outset of the missionary enterprise. Paul spoke of this same calling when he said that he wanted to spend his life preaching the gospel where the name of Christ was not known. He went on three missionary journeys before his incarceration, and he spoke of his desire to go beyond Spain—a dream that was left to Christians after his death.

Ministry to unreached peoples takes many forms. The most common are church planting, translation of the Bible, literacy training and discipleship of young Christians. A lifetime of missionary service to these people could begin with the following steps:

1. Befriend people of other cultures. Develop a lifestyle that celebrates the differences with which God created nations.

2. Begin to focus on one of the major religions mentioned earlier. Become as well acquainted as possible with its beliefs. Try to go beyond textbook learning. If people of that religion live in your region, seek means to become personally involved in their lives and religious activities.

3. And you may want to begin to focus on one country in the world where that religion is well-rooted. Begin to learn everything you can about that nation through books, PBS specials, academic courses, cultural events and neighbors who may be from there. Plan to take a couple of short-term mission trips or vacations to that country. Nothing beats a personal encounter with the culture as a means to cement your heart to that region.

4. Reflect on possible training you could acquire or a vocational track you could enter to prepare yourself to live among unreached peoples. Some countries allow missionaries to come as "missionaries." Other countries do not allow any official missionary involvement. Missionaries enter these societies primarily in the professional work force. They are called tentmakers.

5. If you are currently employed, find out if your company is looking for staff who are interested in taking an assignment abroad. You can often find a three-month to one-year stint that is fully funded by your company. It's a great way to get your feet wet.

6. If you are a student, look for crosscultural academic programs or summer mission projects that are being offered in the country of your interest. This is not only a great way to test God's calling to that particular region, but also it helps you develop a résumé for future employment—you are sending out signals that crosscultural work is important to you.

Environmental Destruction
The call to care for creation has never been so urgent. This generation has

inherited the callous and deadly practices of all the previous generations of time. The condition of our planet has never been as critical as it is today.

Members of Generation X are acutely aware of environmental decay. The language of *ozone, CFCs, rain forests, acid rain, water table,* and *toxic waste* is essentially the vocabulary of this generation. For you, environmental issues are the ultimate prolife concern: if all the world is saturated with poison, there will be no more life; if the great Amazon lungs of the earth are obliterated, there will be no more life. Indeed, entire species are being devastated at a pace that only serves to illustrate the finality of our dilemma.

The sixties generation was the first to seriously grapple with the implications of nuclear war. They were conscious of the fact that for the first time in history, men and women had constructed enough weapons to destroy the entire human race in a matter of hours. And the power to do so lay in the hands of just a few people.

The parallel fact of environmental destruction is the reality of today's generation. The key difference is that the road to annihilation involves the corporate effort and practices of most of humanity. The fault cannot be pinned on a couple of elite persons, corporations or countries. And similarly, the answer to this problem is a community solution. The concerted effort of millions of global citizens who choose to change their personal practices and who influence their employers to change corporate environmental practices is the key to a better planet for the future.

To be sure, the intersection of old practices with environmental concern can take on ridiculous, if not outrageous, dimensions. The U.S. Environmental Protection Agency recently has ruled that all cooling devices on nuclear weapons have to be retroactively fitted with a system that releases fewer CFC's into the environment. Apparently we want to be sure that as we blow entire cities of human beings off the face of the earth, we at least keep the ozone layer intact!

Sadly, we Christians have not led the way in society to care for God's creation. And that is a curious fact, given that creation is literally God's. Many have unfortunately taken a defensive posture on the one hand, conceding environmental concern to New Agers, and many have taken an unbiblical posture on the other hand, preaching that environmental destruction is an acceptable policy, given that all the world must fall apart before Jesus returns. And yet the oldest mandate given to God's family is to care for creation. Faithfulness to this call is at the very least an indication of our respect for the desire and authority of God. The language of lordship in our lives is false if we feel the freedom to bypass this concern of the Creator.

In addition, we lose a most natural bridge to evangelism when we forsake God's call to care for the earth. Millions of global citizens are already convinced of the need to care for creation—they have a part of the truth, even though they may not know the one who made the creation they so admire. We have the opportunity to lead them into a personal relationship with the one who made it all. By contrast, our disregard for the earth deters them from following the one we claim to love, because their natural sensitivities make them recoil from a God who is happy to endorse the blatant destruction of the world. Sometimes it takes people outside the family of faith to give us sight!

There are some simple steps for people who want to take leadership in their lives for creation:

1. Look for ways to "green" your church or fellowship. There are plenty of resources which offer the specifics on everything from recycling to reduction of waste and landscaping. Churches could become great preservation centers each Sunday as members drive up and unload all their recycled goods.

2. Work for the preservation of the rain forests and endangered species. Several organizations are committed to this work. They provide the expertise. All they need is your volunteer time and a little of your money.

3. Build an environmental agenda into your academic and vocational plan. Most major universities now offer sound training that includes crosscultural academic offerings. It makes sense for Christians to look for ways to take leadership in governments and corporations throughout the world, pointing the way to care for the Garden.

4. Build friendships with people inside the environmental movement who are outside the family of faith. Ask God to give you natural and effective

bridges for communication where you can help point the way to the greatest environmentalist of all time. Some churches have committed themselves to evangelistic rallies and personal witnessing at Earth Day events—not as an antagonistic gesture of we-have-it-right, but rather as a friendly call to meet the one who sponsored the original Earth Day.

Ethnic Conflict

The demise of communism in the early 1990s ushered in a moment of euphoria where we thought that world peace was on the brink of "breaking out." The massive enemy of human rights had fallen! Now nations were free to pursue their own individual peaceful courses.

Unfortunately, the fall of communism only liberated decades and generations of ethnic rivalry and conflict that had been suppressed and controlled by the machinery of the state. It's as though seven demons rushed in where one was expelled. Massive ethnic cleansing has reemerged on a level that raises haunting memories of the days of Hitler and a new policy—ethnic dilution—is now in force in parts of Europe where soldiers methodically rape women of other ethnic groups. It is impossible for the redeemed mind to understand the lengths to which human beings will go to assert their imagined superiority and power over others. It's equally inconceivable that the primary progenitors of this ethnic dilution claim to be "Christian." Their victims are Muslims.

Hate crimes are on the increase throughout the Western world as a new level of hostility is being directed toward Jews, blacks and Hispanics. Some sickness in the human composition draws a sense of self-worth from the denigration of others. That condition is as old as time itself and is one of the clearest indications of our need for a Savior to rescue us from the impact of the Fall.

It is only natural to expect Christians to take the lead in celebrating the diversity and beauty of all God's creatures. Human beings are the highlight of God's creative work. As mentioned earlier, we were all conceived in love and are regularly pursued by the everlasting, inexhaustible heart of God. Together we are brothers and sisters in God's family—red, brown, yellow, black and white. None superior to the other, none inferior to the other.

We should not be threatened by people who are different from us. They are God's gift to us for our own enrichment and benefit. Whereas we would expect the natural person to respond out of fear and suspicion, we would expect those who have been redeemed by Christ and filled by the Holy Spirit to operate out of love and acceptance. We are those who welcome the world—in all its diversity—into our lives. We are those who love to point to the unity of the Christian family as a sign of the kingdom of God. The Scriptures teach us that the gospel is always about the work of breaking down the barriers that divide and tear us apart. We have been given the work of reconciliation.

Every level of hostility directed at other groups of human beings—be it in the form of extreme nationalism, racism or sexism—is an offense to the work of Calvary, an insult to the personal effort of Jesus Christ to reconcile the world through his death on the cross. Christians, above anyone else, should be the most vocal in their denunciation of words and deeds that denigrate any of God's people. Ethnic conflict is only going to get worse. It is a critical moment on our fragile globe and members of Generation X will need to step forward to lead the way.

In 1990, thirty Global Project students from various ethnic backgrounds and their Soviet counterparts sat on the stage at a town meeting in the Ukraine. It was a tense moment when the question came, "Isn't there racism in North America? In the USSR, a racially mixed group could never get together except in the army. But you have been smiling! Why?" Before the project director or staff could answer, Stacey, a student on that project, spoke up. As she told of growing up in the housing projects in Atlanta and described what American racism had done, she told of what brought the team together—the living image of God in each of them. The team's witness was strengthened by Stacey's testimony of racial reconciliation on the team.

Stacey wrote to those who provided the scholarship funds for her 1990 trip:

Millions of thanks to my supporters. Your investment in my life made a great impact on my future. Without your help, I wouldn't have seen the move of God in another country or developed friendship with people of different color (race). I have seen God's AWESOME power and have many friends. I also have a desire to stay involved with missionaries and what is going on in other countries. Thanks for blessing me with your love and support.

Here are several beginning steps for people who want to lead in the area of ethnic reconciliation:

1. Work to enlarge your circle of friends to include people who do not look or sound like you. It is natural to cling to "our own kind," and we have to make a concerted effort to do otherwise.

2. Look for cultural events in your area or on PBS that will introduce you to the ways of people who are not from your ethnic group. Learn from their art, music, literature and folklore. Broaden your diet to include their foods.

3. Seek out fellowship in a church that celebrates ethnic diversity, instead of a church that pursues ethnic homogeneity. Work to expand the diversity of your own church of fellowship and to transform racist attitudes and structures.

4. Take as many crosscultural trips as possible. Students can do this with a variety of academic programs, summer mission projects and vacations.

5. Consider relocating to a district of town that does not look like your own ethnic heritage. If this jump looks too frightening, seek out the partnership of friends who will go that route with you.

The Post-Christian Society

We have reached the point in North America where we have moved from our Judeo-Christian roots and have taken on the nature of a post-Christian society. The transition to this state has been gradual but predictable. And we can only fault ourselves, the church, for this shift.

Ever since World War II, society has been asking questions of God. What kind of people are willing to destroy millions of others because of the pride of race? What kind of a world has to build atomic bombs in order to be safe? Why do so many starve to death while so many others die from overconsumption, strangled by their own wealth? Why doesn't society own up to its abuse of indigenous peoples? Why do we not feel compassion when a person dies of AIDS, and yet give a hero's funeral to someone who dies protecting our interests on foreign soil? Why do our presidents lie? Why do we condone racism but condemn left-wing governments?

This is just the beginning of the list. Unfortunately, we Christians have not always provided society with the moral leadership required to survive the pressing issues and dilemmas of the day. Too often we are more willing to support the status quo and condemn those who are asking the honest questions. The risk of telling the truth seems too large. But no society can maintain the basis for its existence after too many prolonged years of unanswered questions. Today, many in society mistrust the church. They do not find in the church a credible or courageous reason for living life. The new society is like a ship afloat without anchor or mooring points. No real worldview has replaced the old. We are still in transition, in that postmodern era where all opinions, preferences and values are equal partners in the domain of truth. We don't know where to settle, and we have no basis to reject one worldview over the other, no compelling reason to proclaim one system as truth above the rest.

Christians can whine about this status of belief in North America—and many do—but we are wrong to do so. We were the physical embodiment of the kingdom to contemporary society and we failed both of them—God's kingdom and society. Indeed, part of the confusion in the church today as we vie for control of public policy and public office is that we do not understand we are no longer a Christian society. We make demands based on our "Judeo-Christian roots," but those arguments and sentiments make no more sense today than the Jewish community in Jesus' day did, making the same demands upon the Roman government for the governance of Jerusalem. Israel had long since lost its moral leadership in the region.

The church must grasp that its role in modern society is much more radical than at any other time in North America's history. Suspicion, mistrust and scorn are the chief filters through which secular society views us. We have the challenge of living out the message of the cross, a gospel of love, service and powerlessness that does not demand rights, but rather models true servanthood.

Society will not accept our intellectual tenets unless our moral life backs them up. Indeed, the diabolical nature of a society that is slipping into a post-Christian era is that it will gravitate toward those selfish values and lifestyle choices that it knows to be wrong and destructive, choices that were earlier restrained by the influence of Christianity. No society honestly believes in its moral right to abuse children and women, to exterminate ethnic minorities, to pursue unbridled comfort at the expense of those who suffer. But when the church stops serving society as a moral agent, society chooses to live out the worst elements of its nature.

It is as though there is an implied social contract between church and society: You model integrity for us and we will restrain ourselves. But when you capitulate, all hell will break loose. This shouldn't surprise us when we understand that God calls us "the salt of the earth" (Mt 5:13). We are the preserving agent. When we have lost our savor, the Scriptures tell us we are of no value and are thrown out to be trampled under foot. And who is it that tramples us underfoot? The answer to that is, quite clearly, the world. We should not be surprised at how embattled we feel today in contemporary society.

Christians who want to go into the post-Christian society and embody the good news can take a few steps:

1. Look for ways to get your finger on the pulse of contemporary society. Movies, book reviews, art shows, university literature classes, dramas, music and TV are helpful entry points.

2. Rather than have other Christians define post-Christian society for you, be careful to build friendships with people who are outside the church. Allow genuine relationships to be your entrance into their worldview. Do not presume to know the answers to their life situation until you are close enough to them to honestly hear their questions.

3. Read the great philosophers. Many of the post-Christian positions have already been articulated by them. Travel through post-Christian Europe. Learn from Christians in that society how they have sought to be the light and salt in the contemporary context. Read the literature of contemporary Christian leaders from those cultures.

The call of the wild upon Generation X is awesome. It is a high calling that will require all the intellect, creativity, hope, love and imagination God provides. The fruit of the Holy Spirit is the equipment for this great challenge, and the body of Christ is the family through which this calling will be fulfilled. The world waits. The devout Muslims, the urban poor, the abused youth, the embattled ethnic minorities, the ravaged earth, the post-Christian society. They wait for you.

This hour belongs to Generation X—and the Lord is calling.

5
The Lord of the Wild

If we choose to respond to the call of the Lord, we are in good company. Jesus, the one who issues the call, has gone before.

He understands the work of love. He was nearly crushed in his heart by the plight of human suffering. He looked out over Jerusalem and wept. He grew weary of his work and the pressing crowds, and so he asked the disciples to take him out on the lake in a boat where he could get away from it all. He was so exhausted that he slept soundly during a storm that nearly drowned him along with his disciples. He faced the temptations of Satan to give up his ministry and give in to the flesh. He was tempted in every way we are. And he was able to persevere to the very end of his calling and to say with his last breath, "It is finished!"

As we prepare to move out into the world in the name of Jesus, it helps if we understand how he saw himself and his mission. In the book of John, Jesus makes several "I am" statements about himself. They ring back to the simple credential God gave Moses as he was calling him into his life work of leading

Israel from captivity into the Promised Land. This awesome and larger-than-life calling required some assurance. "Who are you?" Moses had to ask the Lord as he stood there by the burning bush, contemplating his options to follow or not. God's answer was simple enough: "I AM WHO I AM."

In other words, "God is God, Moses—what else do you require?"

We stand at our own burning bush this hour. It is the same "I AM WHO I AM," calling us to our destiny, the same one who strung the stars over Moses' head that night some five thousand years ago. In some ways, Moses' life foretold the coming of Jesus. Both were called by the Father, both left a place of riches and status to serve the lowly, both faced the certain anger of ruling authorities, both walked through the desert—one for forty years, the other for forty days, and both led the people toward the Promised Land—neither of them crossing that final river with those they led. And now Jesus says to us, "As the Father has sent me, I am sending you" (Jn 20:21).

And so for us, "God is God, what else do you require?"

Yet, fortunately, we have learned volumes about this one called "I AM," volumes that neither Moses nor the thousands of other saints in the Old and New Testaments were able to know. In some ways, their journey of love to all the world required more faith than will be required of us. John's Gospel allows us a glimpse of the "I AM," and we can understand more about the one who calls us into the wild by taking a look at four of those "I am" statements Jesus made about himself.

I Am the Bread of Life

Jesus regularly entered into conversations with the Pharisees. They were looking for ways to trap him into saying things that would turn the people against him. Jesus appeared to enjoy these moments as God-given opportunities to teach those who wanted to know more. The Pharisees always left more confounded and yet more determined to trap Jesus the next time.

This time they insisted that Jesus give some kind of sign to establish that he was from God. "Give us a miracle," they demanded. They proceeded to remind him that God had given the Israelites manna in the desert, "bread from heaven to eat."

What is exceptionally strange about this challenge is that only the day before, Jesus had miraculously fed the five thousand. Jesus does not bother to point out their short memories, nor the folly of their minds. Rather, he goes to the heart of the issue: Moses was able to call down bread from heaven. Indeed, that was a miraculous sign (and he could have interjected that even then, the Israelites regularly disbelieved God).

But that was the small taco, folks. The manna was very temporary; Jesus gives us something eternal: "I am the bread of life." Every society has its staple—rice, plantain, tortillas, potatoes, bread—the food that promises that no matter what razzle-dazzle fancy foodstuffs come and go, we will still be able to be satisfied, our stomachs filled with the basics. When Christ proclaimed himself as the bread of life, the agrarian people listening to him were immediately able to capture the significance of that image. Christ is the staple of our lives. Yes, if Moses' manna was the small taco, this is the whole enchilada!

Jesus pushes the crowd further to help them understand that he is the bread of *everlasting* life. If you want to live forever, you have to eat of Jesus. (He explains that he does not want to lose even one of those the Father has given him. This is another quick glimpse of the scope of Christ's compassion.) So how does one eat the bread of life? Well, Jesus explains, you have to believe that he is the one sent from the Father. But he makes it even more difficult: "This bread is my flesh, which I will give for the life of the world" (Jn 6:51).

The Pharisees are really exasperated now. Has this guy gone nuts? "How can this man give us his flesh to eat?" Is there something poetic going on here? Jesus doesn't let up: "Whoever eats my flesh and drinks my blood has eternal life. . . . For my flesh is real food and my blood is real drink" (Jn 6:54-55).

After this little interaction, the Bible tells us, many of Jesus' followers turned away from him. They were not able to accept his strange words. This is a pattern of Christ in the Bible. He seems to guard the truth enough to keep only the sincere seekers on board. Those who continue with him in faith will eventually be rewarded with understanding.

We have the benefit of the entire Calvary story in the four Gospels and the New Testament letters. We understand that Christ was foretelling his death and laying the groundwork for the gift of eternal life through communion with himself. Christ's body broken for us on Calvary is the true bread and wine. If we are to have the bread of life, the true staple of our spiritual existence, then we must place our trust in Jesus. And we learn from this account that our spirits will hunger, continually looking for satisfaction, if we do not eat the bread of life. All of society's search for satisfaction will only turn out people who are spiritually hungry. As we go into the world, following the call of the "I am," we are bringing to the world the source of eternal life and the secret of a satisfied life.

I Am the Way, the Truth and the Life

Imagine for a moment the vulnerability of the disciples. They have been faithfully following Jesus for three years, not fully sure of the outcome of their loyalty, but certainly aware that they have linked up with a most unusual person. He casts out demons, heals the sick, tells the storm to mellow out, speaks in riddles, feeds thousands, doesn't have a source of regular income, fights with the religious leaders and hangs around with the lowlife. They are not clear in their minds how the whole story is going to end, but the gamble of faith is worth it. Perhaps Jesus is a prophet who will point the way to the ultimate Messiah; perhaps he will lead the liberation uprising against Rome as Moses did for Israel in Egypt.

And then comes the bad news: I'm going to be leaving you soon, I won't be around much longer. And where I am going you cannot come. But don't worry, you will follow me later. Peter, of course, is all ready to get with the program: Hey, Lord, I'm ready to go with you right now, I don't care what the cost is, let me go along. (Sounds like a rookie offering to go along on a hit job.) Jesus' response is not very comforting: You think you can really follow me, Peter? Listen, the truth is, you are going to *deny* me. And then, as if no big deal has just been revealed, "Do not let your hearts be troubled. Trust in God; trust also in me."

Who is this guy?

But Jesus loves his disciples. They have shown their devotion to him, they have stayed with him through the years as others filtered in and out of their ranks. Now he shares with them the really good news:

In my Father's house are many rooms; if it were not so, I would have told you. I am going there to prepare a place for you. And if I go and prepare a place for you, I will come back and take you to be with me that you also may be where I am. You know the way to the place where I am going. (Jn 14:2-4)

The disciples are warmed, but still confounded, and this is where we see the next "I am" picture of Jesus: "I am the way and the truth and the life" (Jn 14:6). Jesus fills this out for his disciples. He explains that the only way to have a relationship with the Father is through himself. Jesus is not only doing the work of the Father—the Father is somehow doing those works through Jesus. And now Jesus will be returning to the Father. To have fellowship with God in heaven will require placing faith in Jesus.

The disciples had caught a glimpse of this truth in the earlier image of the bread of life. Christ is filling it out for them. But he is going even further. For the first time he is explaining to the disciples that they are not just to ask what they can get out of the Father; they cannot just ask to be with Jesus all the time. No, there is a work that he is expecting them to do. That is why he must leave them and prepare a place for them. There will be a time when their work is over and they will need to rest—he is going to prepare that wonderful place for them. Jesus tells them that they will be doing the same amazing works that he himself has been about. And even greater.

Apparently, to accept Jesus as the way to the Father is to also accept the life of Jesus for ourselves. "As the Father has sent me, I am sending you," and "Go into all the world" are the life work of people who have eaten the bread of life. We do not consume the bread just for our own good. We eat in order to feed others. We take in the life of Christ in order to pass it on. We gain the truth in order to share it. We receive the promise of lodging in heaven, and we labor to take as many tenants along with us as we possibly can.

I Am the Light of the World
In another confrontation with the religious leaders (initiated by them again),

a woman caught in adultery is brought before Jesus. What will he suggest they do? The Jewish law stated that such a person should be stoned (and of course, in that sexist society, there was no mention of the man who was caught in the same act). Will Jesus presume to have the authority to pronounce the judgment? Or will he be in favor of ignoring the Law and just allowing the women to go free? It's another attempt to trap Jesus.

Jesus plays their game well. He makes his pronouncement: "If any one of you is without sin, let him be the first to throw a stone" (Jn 8:7). They all slowly slink away, from the oldest to the youngest. None of them would make the blasphemous claim that they are without sin. Fooled again. Jesus then tells the woman that he does not condemn her, and he orders her to go and sin no more. Jesus then takes advantage of another teaching opportunity handed to him by the Pharisees' folly. He makes the radical statement: "I am the light of the world. Whoever follows me will never walk in darkness, but will have the light of life" (Jn 8:12).

The lesson is clear. All of you—this woman and all of you Pharisees alike—are living in darkness. Your double standard is a false one. If you desire to walk in the light, follow me. Jesus is making the unequivocal statement that he is righteousness incarnated. Not only is he the *way* to righteousness, he *is* righteousness. A few sentences later he is telling these Pharisees the chief difference he sees between them:

> You are from below; I am from above. You are of this world; I am not of this world. I told you that you would die in your sins; if you do not believe that I am the one I claim to be, you will indeed die in your sins. (Jn 8:23-24)

We cannot be righteous aside from the work of Jesus in our life. This is not a statement of how to get into heaven. It is a statement of how to become pure. "All our righteous acts are like filthy rags," said the Old Testament prophet Isaiah to the people of Israel (Is 64:6). These learned Pharisees knew that passage well. And now Jesus was telling them that he himself was their only hope of becoming clean.

This is the good news we offer the world. Yes, we are born into the world as children of the deep, condemned to live in darkness, to live out the sinful nature of our flesh. But we can be saved from all of that if we are willing to put our faith in Jesus. This, indeed, is what it means to become a new creation. Once we were instruments of unrighteousness, but now, by the blood of Jesus, we are instruments of good. And if we are to take into account the call to go into all the world as Jesus did, then we are given the insight to understand that God is calling the church to go into all the dark recesses of the world and there proclaim the light of Jesus. We are to continue the ministry of confrontation with the evil one. Where fear is sown, we sow love; where deceit is sown, we sow the truth; where violence rules, we enter in peace; where sorrow reigns, we minister joy; where sin abounds, we usher in the forgiveness and cleansing work of Jesus.

"Let your light shine before men, that they may see your good deeds and praise your Father in heaven," Jesus exhorts us (Mt 5:16). It is our privilege to tell the world, "You do not need to be devastated by darkness, you do not need to die in your sins!"

During the summer of 1990, Marian Carney helped lead a Global Project to Kiev, Ukraine. Her small group had five Americans in it. One was a woman of mixed race, raised by a white family. She had spent her life hating her blackness. Another was African-American. A third was a person whose father literally chased persons of color off his street with his truck. Still another had parents who were obviously prejudiced toward a particular racial group. The last was a missionary kid from Papua New Guinea who had been raised not to describe people by their ethnic differences. Marian, who is a wonderful leader, set out to *not* be a substitute mother for her team members during the summer and to *not* be a person who solved all their problems. She remarked about the fact that her students struggled a great deal in their small group. They had things to work through, including stereotypes of each other. They struggled in their attempts to love one another. They allowed Jesus, the light of the world, to shine into their hearts and their relationships. This influenced their ability to reach out in love to their hosts in Ukraine. God did bless their efforts and their light shone brightly there.

I Am the Good Shepherd
Our final "I am" statement tells us more about the nature of Christ and the

mission to which he calls us. Jesus employs the image of the gate of a sheep pen to remind us that he is the one who serves as the way to the Father. There are those, he tells us, who go around the gate and climb over the fence, but they are counterfeits, robbers. There is only one true shepherd.

Jesus explains the nature of the thief: he comes to steal, kill and destroy. This is a fairly clear statement of Christ's view of those who would claim to be the Messiah! No fuzzy Christology allowed here. Christ, on the other hand, comes that we might have life and have it abundantly. We are not only offered the entrance into life—we are offered the abundance of it. Whereas the thief would take everything from us, including our life, Jesus will provide everything we could ever need.

There is more. Jesus is the *good* shepherd. We can put our trust in this shepherd, we do not need to fear his character. In fact, we learn from this passage that this shepherd lays down his life for his sheep. If an attacker comes to the pen, the shepherd is not going to run off like some hired hand. On the contrary, he will fight if it costs him his very life. This provides a fascinating picture of Calvary. Satan is the wolf who comes to kill and destroy. Christ foils the attack by fighting to the death on the cross. Calvary itself was a war.

We also learn that this shepherd has a relationship with the sheep. They know each other's voice. It is the kind of unity, says Jesus, that is experienced between him and the Father. Jesus is telling us that when we follow him and come under his protection, we are entering into fellowship with the Father— he also knows us. In some ways we are given a glimpse of the church here. It is a community, a family. There is one shepherd and we all have the privilege of being known, together, by the Father.

Jesus offers one final picture of the good shepherd. "I have other sheep that are not of this sheep pen. I must bring them also. They too will listen to my voice, and there shall be one flock and one shepherd" (Jn 10:16). Jesus is concerned that all the sheep of the world come into his pen. This is just another clear reminder of what has been said repeatedly in the New Testament already: God wills that none should perish. Many will reject Christ as Savior. However, all evil will one day be conquered, because finally there will be just one shepherd. Satan, the wolf, and all those other counterfeits will somehow be destroyed. We are given a picture of good triumphing over evil in the end.

Obviously, if we are to imitate the good shepherd, we too will look for other sheep to bring into the fold.

There are many other images of Christ in the Bible. Below we briefly highlight a few more of his characteristics. We want to be well-acquainted with the one who calls us into the wild. We want to know in whose care we rest, but we also want to know how to proceed as we respond to his call.

The Servant

It is an unusual king who makes himself a servant to those over whom he rules. This is what some have referred to as the "upside down kingdom." The passage that most precisely describes God's servanthood to us is Philippians 2:5-11:

Your attitude should be the same as that of Christ Jesus:

Who, being in very nature God,

did not consider equality with God something to be grasped,

but made himself nothing,

taking the very nature of a servant,

being made in human likeness.

And being found in appearance as a man,

he humbled himself

and became obedient to death—even death on a cross!

Therefore God exalted him to the highest place

and gave him the name that is above every name,

that at the name of Jesus every knee should bow,

in heaven and on earth and under the earth,

and every tongue confess that Jesus Christ is Lord,

to the glory of God the Father.

Hyun Joo learned about this call to serving while on a short-term mission trip in a Christian hospital in northern India. "What am I doing to myself?" she wondered, as she dealt with the emotions of fear and loneliness. She was a world away from her family in Philadelphia, her church and her studies at the University of Pennsylvania School of Medicine. Spurred on by her experiences at church and at Urbana 90, she had taken a year off from med school to get a realistic picture of the mission field. She thought of her mother, who had cried for weeks before Hyun Joo left for India. Hyun Joo cried too.

The four-day trip by herself to the hospital "was my bottom-most point" emotionally during her work in India, Hyun Joo recalls. However, God brought her far beyond that point in her experiences. "He taught me how to totally depend on him," she says.

Hyun Joo attends Emmanuel Church in Philadelphia, a Korean-American church affiliated with the Presbyterian Church in America. At Emmanuel, she grew in her faith and understanding and in her interest in missions. It was there that she first heard of the Urbana student mission convention, from friends who attended Urbana 87. With the support of her church, she decided to take advantage of the opportunity.

When she went to Urbana 90, "I wanted to meet God in some way," she recalls. "I felt like he was kind of far away." She remembers that she felt willing to dedicate herself to God, "but a lot of things were holding me back," such as parental opposition, a fear of being sent to a hard place, and a desire for a marriage partner.

At Urbana, God first exposed Hyun Joo's own sin as he convicted her about her own sinful attitudes towards others. As a medical student, "I was especially critical about AIDS patients and drug abusers, to the point that I believed they should die," she says. "But God told me that he loves them, and who was I not to love them?"

She learned that her fears were just excuses—"that if I'm really dedicated to God and willing to do his work, he will solve all the problems," she says. It made her much more willing to serve God.

Urbana "strengthened me in a great way. It encouraged me to go for it."

Hyun Joo visited several exhibitors at Urbana, looking for short-term opportunities related to her medical studies. At home, as she shared her experience with friends and reviewed Urbana 90 audio cassettes and video-tapes, she became convicted to try a short-term experience. "I knew once I graduated it would be another five to seven years before I would have a chance to go anywhere," she says. "I was scared that I might drift away without having a realistic picture of missions."

She also decided that a two-month summer experience would be too short to get a realistic picture of the mission field. Using the Urbana Options Guide in her delegate handbook, she contacted the agencies with needs in the area she was interested in, and wound up choosing SIM International. With the encouragement of her church, Hyun Joo overcame the obstacles to her service. "I can't be any more thankful to my church," Hyun Joo says. "A lot of people were praying for me, and they showed a lot of love through letters and prayers. The whole church was involved."

In India, Hyun Joo got to look at mission work in a way not possible through a summer project. She divided her time between two rural hospitals. At an all-female hospital, she was involved with obstetrics and gynecological cases, delivering babies and doing minor surgical work.

"I don't think I did much for other people, but I learned a lot for myself." It strengthened her relationship with God significantly. "I was able to feel him much closer," she says, through extended times alone at night when she read the Bible. "I was able to see the power of God much clearer than here where everything is blocked by my mentality and orientation and technologies." In the States she had relied on her medical knowledge; in India "there were many cases where I knew the patient would die tomorrow, but it didn't happen. The patient survived. That happened so many times, when all we could do was pray."

Hyun Joo is a changed person through this experience of serving. And has told God she will go with her medical degree wherever he sends her.

At dinner with his disciples one evening, Jesus takes a towel and a basin of water. He proceeds to wash his disciples' feet, a duty usually reserved for the servant of the house, certainly not the master. Christ's message is simple enough to his disciples and to those of us who follow him today. We cannot go into the world as lords. We must go as those who have a hallowed sense of heaven and the humble heart of a slave. The message of the gospel cannot be transmitted through people or organizations that would rule over the spirits and lives of men and women. That is the model we sometimes see in Christian ministries, but it is not God's model. And if we are going to respond to the Lord of the wild, we must go as he did, to serve.

The Lamb

Here's a curious twist: Jesus is not only the Good Shepherd, he is also the Lamb, the one who suffered and was slain for the sake of the world. Jesus stood innocent before Pilate, like a lamb being led to slaughter.

The image of the lamb in the Old Testament was most commonly used to describe the one who took on the sins of the nation of Israel. All the wrong that we commit is transferred to an innocent lamb who is then slaughtered—dies in our place. We become free to serve God, our sins forgiven. Christ was clearly foretold through this Old Testament image, and that is why the Scriptures refer to him as the Lamb of God, slain to take away the sins of the world.

There is a sense in which we are all to become like lambs for the sake of the world. As Christ took on the evil of the world, so too we enter the ravaged, destructive, hating, violent territory of the evil one and bear the darkness for their sake. There is a false sense of "purity" that we are tempted to acquire—it is that feeling that nothing dirty or wicked has brushed against our souls or bodies. We stay away from the den of perdition, the cheats and the prostitutes. But this is not really our right. Jesus placed himself in that world (we know this because the Pharisees accused him of it) and was able to build relationships with people who otherwise were rejected by society. Jesus was able to point them to the light.

Clearly we are not the Lamb of the world, but we are called to follow the Lamb's life. As we go into the world, following the Lord of the wild, we have to adjust ourselves to the idea of taking on the grime, dirt and evil of a lost and crooked generation.

Our Mother

God has both male and female qualities. We learn this from the very first statements about humans: In his image he made us—both male and female. Some Scriptures refer to God as our Father, while other passages call us to the one who would gather us under wing as a mother hen would gather her chicks. Unfortunately, the church has often neglected the feminine images of God. We do an injustice to both God and society when we deny the truth of God's full nature. And we do a particular injustice to women when we deny the full nature of God in them.

We learn from the Bible that God has maternal qualities. God nurtures us in the womb (Is 46:3), gives birth to us (Deut 32:18), protects us in comforting arms (Is 46:3-4; 66:13). We often hear sermons on the father heart of God, and so we should. But we are sadly lacking in a solid treatment of the maternal heart of God. All the warm, tender, nurturing images we have come to associate with mothering are actually the fingerprint of God, the character of our heavenly God. Our moms bear in them the image of God, and by their care of us they teach us about God.

Perhaps the most immediate implication of these maternal characteristics of God is that all the world looks for the coddling care of God. Most of us would like to discover that we were carried in the womb of God with the same kind of love and anticipation that our earthly moms had as they carried us. Most of us would like to know that we have the freedom to approach God with the same boldness we have with our moms—no pretense of "having it all together," no condemnation, no need to hide the tears.

Culture often outpaces the church in terms of moral development. This is true of the women's movement. Christians have been slow to accept women as full equals in the kingdom, and the implications for the gospel have not been good. In some churches, our message to secular women has been that we expect them to become second-rate citizens if they join up with the church. This is not a very attractive offer for women who have been struggling to become first-rate citizens in the culture at large.

There are a few passages that raise questions about a woman's role in the church. But these passages are no more challenging to us than the few end-time verses we use to establish our eschatology. This generation is perhaps the first one that will fully accept women into the church as equals.

A combination of cultural forces and careless biblical work have been the two chief barriers that have kept women held down to this point. In this generation, the church has the culture in its favor, and it needs to take on the serious biblical work of ending the myth that discriminates against women. Society needs to know about the maternal heart of God. And society needs women who can incarnate those maternal qualities at every level of life in our culture and at every level of life in our churches. More than half of the missionary task force throughout recent decades has been female. But not so in church leadership. As one veteran missionary woman puts it: "I was fully free to exercise my gifts on the mission field. But at home, in the U.S.A., I can distribute the bulletins."

Our Healer

If we were to tally all the biblical verses that show the ministry of Christ and then arrange those verses by subject, we would discover that Christ's chief encounter with people on earth was through the ministry of physical healing. Today there are gifted persons who have been given a particular gift of miraculous healing, but they are clearly in the minority.

We could miss the point of healing if we focus exclusively on the body. In both the Old and the New Testaments we gain a picture of a God who is interested in the whole person. Wholeness, or health, is central to the concern of God as he looks upon society. Remember how earlier in the book we described Jesus' ministry to the world as prophesied through Isaiah. That passage is essentially about the *healing* nature of God. This is how it was expressed:

The Spirit of the Sovereign LORD is on me,
>   because the LORD has anointed me
>   to preach good news to the poor.
He has sent me to bind up the brokenhearted,
>   to proclaim freedom for the captives
>   and release from darkness for the prisoners,
to proclaim the year of the LORD's favor
>   and the day of vengeance of our God,
to comfort all who mourn,
>   and provide for those who grieve in Zion—
to bestow on them a crown of beauty

> instead of ashes,
> the oil of gladness
> instead of mourning,
> and a garment of praise
> instead of a spirit of despair. (Is 61:1-3)

Christians are called into a most wonderful ministry. We are asked to follow in the footsteps of Jesus, who looked out for the well-being of the entire person. Despair, depression, injustice, hunger, disease—all of these were important to our Lord and are meant to be important to us. As we go into the world under the direction of the one who calls us into the wild, we go with the heart of one who looks to bring the tenderness of a complete gospel to society. God is the magnificent healer of our souls, emotions, bodies and spirits, and we are called to be the compassionate channels of that healing in today's society—whatever form the healing needs to take.

We cannot expect to be faithful to this calling if we live isolated from the human dilemma. Indeed, we will need to continually seek ways to draw closer to society's pains and heartaches. That is what it means to be incarnational. The world would love to believe there exists a gospel that is wholesome, a gospel that is sensitive to the entire human dilemma, a gospel that is powerful enough to address all the ills of society. We have the privilege of saying in both word and deed, "It's true!"

Our Dignifier

Finally, we discover that this Jesus whom we follow is about the business of returning to people their dignity.

One of the expressions of sin in society is the lie that we are not made in the image of God. We are constantly beaten down with messages of what we need to acquire, what status we need to attain, how we need to change if we are to be acceptable as modern people. The whole goal of Madison Avenue is to convince us that we are not okay, and then to suggest to us certain products that will make us who we ought to be.

This is actually a form of blasphemy. It denies that God's fingerprints are all over us. Certainly we're not fully okay yet—we all have to mature and grow into moral, loving people who reflect the fruit of the Spirit. But this is a far cry from buying certain clothes, watches or cosmetic brands to make us more like Jesus! There is no greater struggle inside the contemporary person than the need to be affirmed, to be liked, to be accepted. And Madison Avenue has done its work well. People are left with the cruel condition of working like crazy to "become somebody," struggling endlessly to deserve the approval of both society and God.

There is no way out of this struggle except the hard work of *believing God*. This sounds simple but it is not. We cannot so easily shake off the years of bad learning, the years of hearing the tapes playing in our heads that say we fall short of dignity. Sadly, many vocational Christian workers are not serving Jesus through a profound gratitude for all he has done for them—too many of them are trying to fill a role which they believe will make them more acceptable to God, trying to do work which they believe will affirm their basic worth.

We cannot buy our worth with deeds. We cannot dress ourselves outwardly with dignity. Our worth is a fact. It comes to us externally by the hand of God and has absolutely nothing to do with us. The fact of our dignity finds its home in our innermost person, and that is the place where we have to experience conversion, a special work of Christ. And this is countercultural in every sense. Every prop that society, the church, our friends, our job (including our ministry), and our most significant other person may offer us, in the pursuit of our dignity, is nothing more than that—a prop.

We spoke earlier of the Pharisees' condemnation of Jesus for hanging around certain kinds of people. These religious leaders carried a high view of themselves and considered the majority of God's people "beneath" them. This double standard is both false and evil; it drew the seething condemnation of Jesus. The church cannot accept those categories. We have to be the community that opens our arms to everyone, that welcomes every human being into our corporate life as a full member, that affirms each person as the miraculous creation of God. The Lord who issued the call to the wild is the same Lord who said, "Whatever you did for one of the least of these brothers of mine, you did for me" (Mt 25:40).

6
Personal Frontiers in the Romance

God's economy of life operates in such a fashion that whatever he calls us to—for the benefit of others—is also good for our own benefit. We cannot always understand this truth through our natural mind. How can we explain the call to carry our cross, to follow Christ to the point of death, to give up our rights, as beneficial? We can only understand this great mystery through the eyes of faith.

And this, in fact, is how the entire life of discipleship works.

Did you ever think, "If I could just be *sure* things will work out if I follow Christ . . ."? That assurance just is not given to us. We are called to live by faith.

It is the picture of the Israelites escaping Egypt. Pharaoh's army is fast approaching from the rear. Captivity is sure to be cruel and deadly. But ahead is the Red Sea. Moses has stretched his rod over the waters and they have rolled back to form mighty walls. But they could easily come crashing down.

What to do? Surrender to Pharaoh does offer some security: at least there is likely to be housing and food in exchange for hard labor. The price, of course, is to give up freedom and settle for slavery. Yet to step into the sand and walk between the walls of water is an uncharted path. There's no instruction manual, no guarantee, no video shots of thousands of others who have gone before. It's a risk, and the reward on the other side is the Promised Land.

The choice faced by the Israelites that day was no different from the choice we face today as we consider the Lord's call to us: to live by faith, to step into the wild and usher many into the Promised Land. We are tempted to accept the compromise of the modern-day Pharaoh: Go for the job, the house, the status, the security. Sure, we lose our souls, but, as the bumper sticker says, "He who dies with the most toys wins."

We know, though, how false that is. God didn't create us to live divorced from our souls. "What good is it for a man to gain the whole world, yet forfeit his soul?" Jesus asks (Mk 8:36). The answer is an obvious zero. The choice is not between security and faith. It is between death and life.

There is a personal price for going with God's love story. Jesus never called people to follow him without first warning them to consider the cost. In fact, he seemed to regularly turn people away because he didn't want impulsive decisions for the kingdom. If you are going to build a house, Jesus warned, be sure you have the money in the bank to complete the structure. If you are going to war against another nation, first be sure your army is capable of victory.

Each of us has our own frontiers of faith, our own personal areas of challenge to grow and trust God. And there are several frontiers of faith that are common to all of our walks with Christ. We'll focus on those for the rest of this chapter.

Love
The golden thread of life, as we said earlier, is the love of God. The great Lover is romancing the globe, and we have been called into partnership with Christ in this global work.

As simple and as strange as it may sound, the first and most important frontier of faith that confronts us is the question: "Will we fall in love with God?"

There are at least three elements to this question. The first has to do with *the wholesome love of God.*

We have seen how God loves the entire person—he reaches in to heal our wounds, our souls, our spirits. Where there is grieving, God brings joy; where there are sin and destruction, God brings forgiveness and another chance. Scripture demonstrates that God loves the orphan, the widow, the hungry, the prisoner and the sick. No level or category of the human dilemma falls outside the scope of God's love—it is complete, it is perfect.

The step of faith for us, then, is to let the wholesome love of God go to work in our own lives. Many of us have been taught to see God's love as primarily a doctrinal concept, something that is responded to with a prayer to "receive Christ into our hearts." And it is that, but that is just the beginning. God desires to reach deep into each of us and love us at every level of our personal pain. We are being asked to become vulnerable in this relationship with God. The personal pain that we carry with us may include child abuse, sexual assault, rejection, divorce, death, abandonment. It may seem "safe" for us to remain in the privacy of our hurts and not venture out into relationships in ways that make us vulnerable to pain once again. And yet God requires us to share in others' pain if we are to truly receive his love.

We spoke earlier of a secure self who is known and loved by God in the inner person. This is what the work of love does for us. It can be a very long and difficult road, but there is no shortcut, no other way to health than to come to understand and accept God's love. Through this journey God is able to heal us in our inner self, make us mature and satisfied in his love. We become people who are exceptionally content and stable, capable of leading others to the healing work of Christ. It is accurate to say that the degree to which we have personally experienced the wholesome, loving work of God in our lives will become the degree to which we can lead others into a loving relationship with Christ. This truth underscores the fact that our duty is not primarily a doctrinal one. If it were, we could simply "tell" people what we have learned about Christ. What we in fact are supposed to do is invite others to join us in the personal adventure of falling in love with Jesus.

One of my struggles (Dan speaking) throughout life has been with anger. It has resulted in my being verbally abusive with my family at times. I'm embarrassed to acknowledge this, but it is true. A couple of years ago, during a period when my wife was getting some counseling and growing significantly through it, she made the suggestion that perhaps one of the sources of my anger was the sexual abuse in my childhood (which we had talked about). This was a brand-new thought to me, so I reached out to a Christian counselor for help.

It took some time before the counselor was able to help me explore this memory, but eventually she did. When I was a boy, the organist in my church invited me to his apartment to enjoy his studio-quality stereo equipment. This man was a homosexual and abused me.

It was my brother who, when he learned about this situation, got me out of it. As far as I know, nothing ever happened to the man. The depths of the impact of that abuse on me I will never fully understand until I am with the Lord. I always felt that I was responsible for getting into that situation because I enjoyed jazz. The impact on my sense of who I am was profound. Insecurity has been one of the terrible consequences of this abuse.

I thank God, however, for my healing. This is not to suggest that there are no residual negative consequences of that sexual abuse, but only to say that · by God's grace I have made significant progress in managing my angry feelings and conveying them in healthy, appropriate ways—ways that are less destructive to those around me. God's love meets us in our personal pain.

The second area of our lives where this call to love must go to work is in *our need for forgiveness.*

All of us carry a history of sinning that requires the cleansing work of Christ. But we sometimes fear going to God with these issues. The reason is that we feel condemned by our deeds. We are in bondage. Satan is the great deceiver. He tricks many of us into believing that God condemns us for our past. If Satan can immobilize us with this overwhelming sense of guilt, we become useless to the kingdom. What we need to know is that "there is now no condemnation for those who are in Christ Jesus." That is right out of the Bible—Romans 8:1.

Christ approaches us with conviction, not condemnation. Whereas condemnation ends the relationship, conviction asks that the relationship continue. The role of conviction is to point out where something is blocking our relationship with Christ so it can be dealt with. When Christ asks, "Will you let me love you?" he is inviting us into intimacy. Sin blocks that intimacy in the same way as infidelity blocks intimacy between a man and a woman. God wants us to trust his character and go through the work of being reconciled to him. He approaches our sins with the care and gentleness of an expert surgeon who deftly cuts out the offending tissue in our bodies. He does not come to us with a chain saw. To be sure, we have to expect that there may be pain in the work of being reconciled. That is part of the natural consequence of having sinned against God and others. But if we cannot trust God in this area of our lives—as an ongoing reality—we cannot expect to have the privilege of inviting others to experience the ongoing goodness of God either.

We share with you this honest and vulnerable letter which a student wrote:
I am writing to share with you the wonderful experience I had as a delegate at Urbana 90. It came at a time when I was about to reject God altogether. I didn't want to go to Urbana, but I had to because I'd already registered and made plans. I knew it was all about Christ's healing for our broken world. Feeling that God would never use me, I was bracing myself for a week of bitterness, seeing others joyfully inspired to spread the gospel while I was cursed by God. In one sense, I was right—God couldn't use me—*as I was.* But what I didn't expect was that I would, myself, receive Christ's healing power and grace as I never thought I could.

For nine years I was gay. Five of these I was a Christian. I knew that homosexuality was sinful; yet I also "knew" that it was so much a part of me that it was impossible for me to change. As the years went on and as I grew in Christ, this became more and more of an obstacle in my knowing God. I found it impossible to reconcile the fact that I was "stuck with" this sinful nature with the fact that God desires us to be holy, and that Christ cannot live where there is sin. I can never be holy, I thought. God has rejected me and cursed me; and I began to reject and curse God.

How little I understood! Of course, I was right in one sense—God was *not* able to use me (at least not very fully)—*in my present state.* What I lacked was the faith that God *could* and *would* wrench even this sin from my grip if I gave him the slightest chance. How I clung to it! How frightened I was that he might actually take it away, and I would be an entirely different person! On the eve of the New Year, I gave Jesus just that slight chance he needed. "I believe you have the power to remove this from my life," I told him. "And I haven't any idea what will become of me if you do. But right now I am willing to trust you. So do what you must quickly, before I change my mind." Jesus took it and began a healing in me that is the most glorious thing I've ever experienced. I *am* a different person, just as I had feared I would be! But I have picked up the business of following him once more, faithful—much more faithful—this time, faithful always. The power of Jesus, the grace, and the love are overwhelming to me.

Five months later, I feel like a patient returned to normal life after months in a hospital, but who feels better than ever knowing that a fatal cancer was successfully removed. The surgery—fearful though it was—saved my life! I want to sing and dance and run to Jesus as fast as I can, and I can't get enough of the Word! It is truly by amazing grace.

The third area in which God meets us in love is in *our competing passions.*

God is a jealous lover. The price of a deeper relationship with him will be turning over to him our wayward passions. God wants full reign, complete allegiance. We may be surprised to discover what those passions are, but most often they appear as pride of race, religion, country or gender. Or said in a different way, racism, religiosity, nationalism and sexism.

God has to meet us in each of these areas. These competing passions debilitate us and harm our ability to love the world in Christ's name. Racism obscures the dignity of all God's creatures and gives us a false sense of having the right to lord it over people of another ethnic group. Religiosity elevates our particular brand of Christianity as the "right one" and hinders our fellowship with believers from other traditions. It prevents us from modeling the love of Christ in such a way that people will know we are Christians by seeing the way we love. Nationalism puts "our" country above "theirs" and denies the truth that in God's love there is no east or west and that every nation, tribe and even language will be represented at the final banquet in heaven. Sexism impacts us the same way our racism does, and it locks out half of God's people from their rightful place of service.

The Moscow team sent by the International Fellowship of Evangelical Students (of which InterVarsity is a sister movement) included seven pioneers from six different countries: Denmark, Germany, England, Croatia, Syria and the United States. Diversity? You bet! All seven members came out of student movements such as InterVarsity. Some of them became Christians while in the university; others were Christians before that. All of them were committed to the goal of seeing established an indigenous student movement in Russia. Pursuing that goal together, they had to live and work in harmony. They had to learn how to put the others' interests ahead of their own. They had to look past the differences that divide. The overall impact of their witness was powerful—largely because of their diversity.

One final reflection on the call of love. There is a *counterfeit love* that hurts many of us.

It is a kind of dependency we thrust upon others, a dependency that comes from a deep immaturity and a history of abuse. We want others to take care of us, to tell us what to do, to "make it all better." We do not set appropriate boundaries and are easily influenced and used by others to achieve their ends. All the while we are feeling loved by them because of the attention we receive. Our own "self" becomes completely submerged or lost, and we are no longer genuine people.

We are capable of this same confused relationship with God. Jesus is not asking us to erase our "self." True love does not make that kind of request. Rather, he wants us to rediscover our true self and bring it into the loving relationship with him. God wants us to continually blossom and mature into a self that is expressing its full potential—into a self that is saying yes to the relationship with Christ not because of our extreme need, but because of our free choice to pursue love in a deep and mature exchange.

Lordship

Imagine the audacity of a New Testament slave who, after being bought in the marketplace, announces to his master that he will be taking a few years off to pursue his own plans. The idea would have been laughable, and if he pursued it the slave would have met with certain death. Slaves were entirely the property of their owners, in the same way as a cow or a plow. These were all implements in the hands of the master and their exclusive purpose was to fulfill the desires of the owner. The Bible doesn't approve of this system, but it does report it.

The Scriptures tell us that we, too, were bought at a price—the blood of Calvary. We are now slaves of righteousness rather than slaves of evil. This image may seem harsh to us, but it is biblical. Even though the primary motivation for all our service to Christ and the world is the high calling of love, there is the picture of *lordship* throughout the Bible, a reflection of the fact that we do not belong to ourselves. It is important to understand the implication of this truth along with the call to love. As we look at the personal frontiers of growth necessary to follow Christ into all the world, we see each of them touched by lordship.

An important lordship issue for us in this book is the "harvest," and there are two ways to apply this truth. The first is that *God, the Lord of the harvest, is primarily responsible for the work.* We are easily crushed and over- whelmed by the size of the harvest. The fields present more needs than we could ever imagine meeting, and the complexity of the needs is beyond our comprehension. We could easily suffer from paralysis due to the immensity of it all. And if we feel the weight of responsibility as though the entire task of global love rests upon our shoulders, that will certainly freeze up our bodies and souls. But we are not finally responsible for the harvest. Only God is. We are like the slave who lives under the domain of the owner. Our Lord carries the entire burden. We are responsible only for that part he puts in front of us. And remember how many he has called into that harvest.

In part, to practice the lordship of Christ means to let the harvest rest in his hands. If we are not able to do this, then we suffer from an ego problem. We are projecting ourself into the role of God as though somehow all creation centers on our personal actions. We need to humble ourselves and accept a more biblical view of who we are. With Christ as the Lord of the harvest, we have the privilege of working in his fields, knowing that he carries the burden of love more severely than we, knowing that we are actually partners with him in his task. We go to rest at night. He "will neither slumber nor sleep" (Ps 121:4). What *is* our part? To draw near to him in relationship, in order to understand what he is asking of us. A detached or distant walk with Christ will render us incapable of knowing our specific part in the great harvest.

The second implication is the more difficult. If Christ is the Lord of the harvest and if he is the Lord of our lives, then *we have no choice but to labor in the harvest.* We do not have the right to accept the benefits of Calvary and then walk away from the demands of the harvest. To be Christian is to be involved in God's global harvest.

As a senior at Cornell (Dan speaking), I was very much involved in the InterVarsity chapter and in our local church. In both places we had a lot of contact with members of Wycliffe Bible Translators who were doing graduate studies in linguistics and anthropology. Each of them attempted to recruit my wife, Shelby, and me. One couple, Karl and Joyce Franklin from Papua New Guinea, simply made friends with us. We came to love one another and spent a lot of time together. We enjoyed similar entertainment and we laughed a lot together. Quite naturally, they shared with us from their experience in Papua New Guinea, their love for that country, the Kewa people, the progress of their Bible translation effort and so on.

Halfway through the school year, the Franklins showed us a letter from the Wycliffe director in Papua New Guinea, which included a paragraph saying they desperately needed two people to teach at the missionaries' school there. That sounded for all the world like us! They left this letter with us and went out of town for the weekend. We started thinking. And we gathered a whole list of questions that we wanted answered.

As soon as the Franklins returned, we went over our list with them. We got our answers and decided to apply. The following summer we went to the linguistic training school. We joined Wycliffe during the summer of 1964.

Now, as a missionary kid, I had come to the conclusion that I would never find myself compatible with a mission agency. I had fairly strong views on how missionary parents should carry out their responsibilities to their children, and I objected to some of the policies of certain mission agencies. Shelby and I had concluded that we should prepare ourselves to teach in a university somewhere in Asia, more or less as tentmakers. At this point at Cornell, we had two immediate invitations to teach at Asian universities upon my graduation.

At the encouragement of my mentor, Dr. Arthur Glasser, who was then with Overseas Missionary Fellowship, I had explored the possibility of serving with my parents' mission agency. We had also written to several others. One had responded by saying they could find work for Shelby, as a science teacher, but they didn't know what to do with me, a sociology and anthropology major. The more we looked into the policies of Wycliffe, the more compatible we found ourselves with that organization and its policies.

We did not experience a voice from the clouds or a Macedonian call, like Paul the apostle. The opportunity to teach missionary kids seemed to make sense in some ways—seemed to match our sense of our abilities and gifts. We said, "Lord, we don't know what you want us to do. Going to Papua New Guinea is not the direction we have been moving. [Having been born in China among the Tibetan people, I was naturally drawn to Continental Asia.] However, we are going to move in this direction and trust you to confirm our decision—or to close the door if this is not pleasing to you." The Lord immediately began to confirm our decision. (As we look back now on our almost ten years in Papua New Guinea, it is clear that God wanted us to go there and prospered our ministry during those years.)

Shelby and I went to my father telling him of our thoughts of going to teach the Bible translators' children. My father was a contemporary of the founder of Wycliffe, Uncle Cam Townsend, and he had followed Mr. Townsend's ministry over the years. My dad's approach to missions was in many ways similar to the Wycliffe approach.

We asked my dad his opinion and sought his blessing. Typically, Dad would take a request such as that, pray about it for a few days, and then come back with his perspective. But this time, he immediately threw his big arms around both of us, expressed his pleasure with the decision and gave us his blessing. We were on our way.

We shared our new sense of call with our local church, one we had joined when I became a student at Cornell. That university church almost immediately began to double its monthly missions commitment in order to give $150 a month to the support of the Harrisons. Additional proof that the Lord was in this decision.

Our pastor called a number of his seminary classmates and helped us organize an itinerary for speaking to churches, as part of the means for raising our support. With Shelby seven months pregnant, we traveled six thousand miles and spoke in nineteen churches, all in a period of six weeks. When we left for the field, we didn't know whether we had our support, but we were absolutely convinced that we had made the right decision.

Cooperating with the Lord of the harvest means having a no-nonsense vision of life that fights for the pure gold. It's a struggle, a battle of the heart, a duel for the pearl of great price. Listen to the Bible's account of some who have gone for the gold:

> [They] were tortured and refused to be released, so that they might gain a better resurrection. Some faced jeers and flogging, while still others were chained and put in prison. They were stoned; they were sawed in two; they were put to death by the sword. They went about in sheepskins and goatskins, destitute, persecuted and mistreated. (Heb 11:35-37)

And listen to the high compliment God gives them:

> The world was not worthy of them. (Heb 11:38)

The work of love calls us to be disciplined men and women who are willing to keep on going, men and women who see the cost of love and nevertheless persist, who see the rewards of comfort but choose the price of Calvary, who see the pain of society and choose to endure the inconvenience, long hours, sickness, disappointments, violence, failures and cruelty that come with bringing tenderness into those places of pain.

Community

The final personal frontier we address is the body of Christ. Whether we like it or not, God has made all of us who follow the Savior into one worldwide, eternity-long family.

Much in our culture has taught us to believe in the self-made person. As Western Christians, we tend to glorify the individual: "There's nothing that God and I together can't handle." And we model the notion that independence from other human beings is the desired expression of maturity: "No, I wouldn't ask to borrow a mower—I don't like to be indebted to anyone. I went out and bought my own." "No, I don't lend my car. I want to be a good steward of what God has given me."

There can be no question that each of us has to make personal decisions regarding our journey with Christ. No one can decide for us to make Jesus our Lord, no one can decide for us to commit our lives to the task of loving the world. But we cannot take our individualism much farther than that.

This book has been calling us to the biblical notion that we are to live out our faith in the context of human society—to the idea that all the world is our parish. An equally important book could be written regarding the fact that God has called us to live out our faith in relationship to the rest of the body. God began with a couple—it was not good for man to be alone. Eventually he calls a family to become his instrument through whom all the families of the earth will be blessed. This family is to model the corporate life of loving Yahweh. The family grows into the nation Israel—the "people of God," and once again it is through this people that God will demonstrate his goodness to the world. Upon Christ's death a new family is born—the family of Christ. As believers, we are the new spiritual children of Abraham, and it is through our corporate life that God will display his tenderness, forgiveness, reconciliation, justice and hope to the world. *We do not have the right to disengage ourselves from our spiritual brothers and sisters.*

We need to consciously link ourselves to the community of faith in two ways. The first has to do with the diversity of gifts. God says that we are all linked to each other as one body, and that each part contributes something unique to the others. Some have a more public role, others more private. But absolutely no contribution is deemed insignificant in God's view. We are all at loss when one part is not functioning.

During the summer vacations while in Papua New Guinea, we would spend time out in the tribal areas. In the summer of 1972 we were in Usa, in the southern highlands, with the Kewa people. The Franklins were out of the country. They had asked us to encourage the literacy program, and this required us to live in the village setting on our own.

Each day literacy students came to the Bible house. Kewa teachers helped them make progress in learning how to read. One of the Kewa teachers was a man by the name of Truasu, a person we had gotten to know and love. Truasu was a man in his thirties who, for most of his life, had pursued one goal: to find the man who had killed his father when Truasu was five years old, and to kill that man. Truasu knew the man was from a village over the hill. Around the fire every night, he would talk with the elders about how one figures out who committed a crime like this and various strategies for revenge.

However, Truasu happened to be one of the folks who had worked with Karl and Joyce in the translation process. Over the months and years of dealing with the Scripture text, Truasu had been confronted with the Word of God. God had said it was wrong to hate your enemies. In fact, you were to love your enemy. Over time, this made a profound impact on Truasu, and eventually he became a Christian. Truasu became one of the most fluent readers and eventually a very fine teacher.

The leaders of Usa had repeatedly invited men from Puti, the village over the hill, to come down to the Bible house to hear God's talk and to learn how to read the book containing his words.

One morning while we were in Usa, the men from Puti came into the village. You could feel the tension—the Puti men were terrified at coming into Usa. The Usa men were also frightened because the Puti warriors had their bows and arrows, spears and shields with them. When it was determined that the Puti men had come in response to the invitation, things warmed up considerably.

I remember seeing Truasu sit down beside the man he believed had killed his father. He began to share with him about God's love and to teach him the beginnings of how to read the Bible. The power of God's reconciliation upon those believers in Usa and the love of the Lord Jesus through that community of his men and women drew the men from Puti into that potentially dangerous situation in order to learn more about God's truth.

We have to become proactive in applying the truth of the body to our lives. Some of us have personalities and skills that make listening to and learning from others difficult. We are used to listening to our own voice, trusting it to instruct us. But we are deficient if we don't bring other voices into our lives. God's will and the signs of the day are usually revealed to us in the context of listening to God *with others.*

Those with public gifts need to take serious inventory of how they are letting others speak into their lives. On the other hand, those with quiet personalities need to learn to love the community of faith by making their contribution to it. As God provides insights and wisdom, these need to be offered to the rest of the family. Another temptation faced by people with the quieter gifts is to equate noise and flash with leadership or maturity. We must be careful not to relinquish our opinions or decisions to others simply because they are better at being up front. God holds each of us accountable for the talents he has placed in our care, and we cannot abandon them to others.

Community is not expressed only in the gifts. It is also expressed in diversity. God has given birth to a wonderful human family of many colors and cultures. All of these are valuable to the global work of Christ. Part of the miracle of how God created the body is its dependence on other parts for healthy functioning. Inside different cultures are locked special aspects of the kingdom. Each society brings its own peculiar history and values to the Bible and discovers characteristics of the gospel that other groups too can benefit from. We should be looking for ways to connect with these other cultures.

When we separate ourselves from other cultures, it is as though we eat at a delicious salad bar each day—but take only the white dinner roll onto our plate. We have not discovered the delight of dipping into the rest of the salad bar. Neither do we realize that we are slowly becoming dangerously malnourished. And this is precisely what we are doing when we isolate ourselves from the diversity of God's family—we have not discovered the delight of

the human family, and worse, we are slowly becoming spiritually malnourished. And long-term malnutrition is dangerous to our souls. The church is
larger in the Two-Thirds World than it is in the West. It is not possible or
right to live our Christian lives or do our missionary work in isolation from
the rest of the body.

As we close this chapter it is helpful to look at one more biblical picture.
Yahweh was continually working to bring Israel back into relationship with
him. The prophet Ezekiel speaks to the Israelites when they are in captivity,
announcing God's desire to bring them back into the Promised Land, but
warning them that they need to be faithful to the ways of Yahweh if they
return:

> They will return to it [the land] and remove all its vile images and
> detestable idols. I will give them an undivided heart and put a new spirit
> in them; I will remove from them their heart of stone and give them a heart
> of flesh. Then they will follow my decrees and be careful to keep my laws.
> They will be my people, and I will be their God. But as for those whose
> hearts are devoted to their vile images and detestable idols, I will bring
> down on their own heads what they have done, declares the Sovereign
> LORD. (Ezek 11:18-21)

Notice the progression of ideas here. Israel has to make a lordship decision
regarding its history of sin. The people have to make a clean sweep of it,
going through the countryside and destroying all the idols. This is the clear
statement of their decision to go God's way. We face that same question of
lordship.

God promises three wonderful gifts in exchange for this act of lordship.
He will give Israel an undivided heart—the ability to become singular and
pure in their devotion to him. No more wandering-heart syndrome. He will
also give them a new spirit. They'll become new persons, putting away the
spirit of despair, hopelessness and sorrow, receiving in return the spirit of
courage, hope and joy. And then he takes out their heart of stone and replaces
it with a heart of flesh. No longer will Israel live untouched by the pain of
the world. Whereas people could brush against this heart of stone and leave
Israel unmoved, now they will bump against a tender heart and the nation

will move to respond in compassion. Israel will be given the natural ability to love the world in a way that fits their original calling via Abraham and Sarah—the calling to bless the nations. We are offered the same marvelous promise: a new heart and a right spirit.

Then comes the final statement of relationship. If we do *not* clear out the land of its idols, we will experience the judgment and distance of God. Our own detestable behavior will come back to destroy us. (Don't misread this as vindictive; read it as the natural consequence of doing evil.) On the other hand, if we step forward, as followers of God, we will enjoy the wonderful title *My People*. God is claiming us as his community. There couldn't be a greater gift.

7
Pathway to the Wild

So, how do I take on a life of loving the world?

We have focused on the need for believers to show forth the character of Christ—which in our minds is the chief means through which we serve the globe. But there is more. In this chapter we offer practical steps for choosing to live a life fashioned after God's heart for the world. Lots of vocational options go with this kind of call, and a good number of personal issues too. We would emphasize at the start that there is a basic decision to be made. It is simply this: *I choose to be a lifelong activist for the global mission of Jesus.* All of us are capable of making this choice. It requires no sophisticated knowledge of missionary work—it simply requires a heart that has been captured by the compassion of Jesus.

This prayer, this commitment, serves to filter out all the noise that would influence us in other directions. It keeps us focused when we begin to face new options for life. It helps clarify the issues when we find ourselves being seduced into a life of comfort and detachment. Our checkpoint becomes: Do these options or opportunities reflect a life committed to the global mission of Jesus?

The way of discipleship is not a straight line from beginning to end. It is filled with twists, blind curves, the "valley of the shadow of death" and much more. As we follow the global call of God upon our lives, it is good to know that we do not have a map showing our career path. Rather, we are called to an adventure of faith. And that will change the very core of our lives, as we become a lifelong activist for the global mission of Jesus. No two people will walk the same path, because God is working through each of our individual personalities and particular circumstances.

Scott and Janine Bessenecker became Christians while students. After graduating, they married and then Scott came to work for InterVarsity Missions in the Global Project department (previously called Overseas Training Camp). Scott was a clerk and assisted the director in serving the project directors for each of the OTCs. Scott served in that capacity for two years, after which he was promoted to the position of executive assistant. Then he assisted me (Dan) as director of Urbana through the convention. I remember approaching Scott about another promotion to direct the Global Project Department. I said, "It's contingent on one thing, namely at least a three-year commitment."

You didn't have to spend much time with Scott and Janine to realize they were young people who were committed to Christ as Savior and Lord. The world mission of the church drew them, and that commitment seemed to be a permanent one. Their commitment to missions helped them lead two Global Projects to Eastern Europe before the Berlin wall came down. It also made them available as leaders in their local church.

However, when I asked him to make a three-year commitment he said to me, "Three years seems like an awful long time."

Now, there is nothing shallow or inadequate about Scott's sense of commitment. But he is a "twentysomething" person who has grown up in a rapidly changing world and has experienced the lack of permanence in relationships and circumstances today. He therefore defines commitment differently than my generation does. How can he be sure he'll want to stick with something for three whole years?

Scott did commit himself to stay in this new position through Urbana 93, and I suspect he and Janine will be involved in world mission all their lives.

Be a Biblical Person

We have to make the fundamental decision to *become biblical people.* We live in a day of competing philosophies of life as East meets West, modern meets classical and New Age meets old age.

There are compelling elements of truth and reasoning in just about every system of thought in the world. Christians who take on Jesus' global mission need to be students of the Word. We cannot presume to safely tread the philosophical mine field if we have not made the study of the Word central to our weekly routine. The Bible tells us to go into the world as "wise as serpents" (Mt 10:16 RSV), able to give defense for our beliefs both "in season and out of season" (2 Tim 4:2).

This is not just a call to memorize certain verses or "pop-up" answers to contemporary questions or statements that appear to challenge the view of Christianity. It is this but much more. Christians need to become so steeped in the Word that we take on a biblical worldview, a comprehensive orientation of what it means to be Christian—dealing with all of life, from creation to family to citizenship to global ethics. Any goal short of this is folly for people who want to provide leadership in a world governed by fuzzy and dangerous thinking. We live in a world that does not know how to define family, how to argue against racial exclusivity, how to offer sexual guidance to youth, how to treat children in the womb, how to distinguish between entertainment and violence, how to denounce injustice. Society needs clear, compelling, ethical leadership—and we will be powerless to provide it if we do not fall in love with the Word of God.

The Bible is "a lamp to my feet and a light for my path" (Ps 119:105). David, a man described as one after God's own heart, said, "I have hidden your word in my heart" (Ps 119:11). The whole of Psalm 119 is a wonderful statement of loving the Word. It provides us the picture of one who found sustenance and life itself through the regular ingestion of Scripture. We need to take some specific steps if we are to become biblical people. Here are a few suggestions.

First, begin a regular lifestyle of daily quiet times. The Bible tells us that it was Jesus' pattern to draw away each day. We need to find personal means to take in a regular diet of the Bible, meditating on the only written record God has given us about himself. We need to understand that we actually become malnourished if we don't take in this regular diet. Reading the Word each day should be as natural as eating or brushing our teeth. We literally become transformed by the "renewing of our minds" through this regular encounter with God's record; there is absolutely no substitute for it.

Second, we need to take in regular sessions of studying the Word with other Christians. This community approach reflects the spirit of the New Testament church: "every day they continued to meet together" (Acts 2:46). We need other people to help us hear the words of God. We have all been told of the multifaceted, diamondlike nature of the Scripture and the fact that we cannot "see" all of it from our angle. Part of the mysterious nature of the Word is that it cannot fully come to life outside of the context of relationships. It's as though community is the yeast, the life that prompts the Holy Spirit to unveil the Bible to us.

And we also need to acquire advanced training in the Word. There are many ways to go about this—correspondence courses, books, evening classes, Bible college, Christian college or seminary. However we go about it, it makes sense that over a period of several years we complete academic study that gives us a better understanding of the context in which the Bible was written, the main themes that make up its diverse books, the key social issues it addresses and the history of the church's response to these themes and issues. The Bible's compassionate edge should be second nature to us, and there is no way to acquire that without in-depth, concentrated study.

Be a Person of Prayer

We also need to learn to pray, to be sensitive to the Lord's nudges, to become people who regularly spend time at the throne. (An excellent prayer tool for daily use is the book *Operation World*.)

A missionary, home on furlough, told this true story while visiting his home church in Michigan.

While serving at a small field hospital in Africa, every two weeks I traveled by bicycle through the jungle to a nearby city for supplies. This was a journey of two days which required camping overnight at the halfway point. On one of these journeys, I arrived in the city where I planned to collect money from a bank, purchase medicine and supplies, and then begin my two-day journey back to the field hospital. Upon arrival in the city, I observed two men fighting, one of whom had been seriously injured. I treated him for his injuries and at the same time witnessed to him of the Lord Jesus Christ. I then traveled two days, camping overnight, and arrived home without incident.

Two weeks later I repeated my journey. Upon arriving in the city, I was approached by the young man I had treated two weeks earlier. He told me that he had known I carried money and medicines. He said, "Some friends and I followed you into the jungle, knowing that you would camp overnight. We planned to kill you and take your money and drugs. But just as we were about to move in to your campsite, we saw that you were surrounded by twenty-six armed guards."

At this I laughed and said that I was certainly all alone out in that jungle campsite. The young man pressed the point, however, and said, "No, sir, I was not the only person to see the guards. My five friends also saw them, and we all counted them. It was because of those guards that we were afraid and left you alone."

At this point in the church presentation in Michigan, one of the men in the church jumped to his feet and interrupted the speaker. He asked, "Sir, can you tell me the exact day that this incident happened?" It took the missionary a moment to recall, but he could. When he informed the congregation of the date, the man who had interrupted him told this story: "When it is night in Africa, it is day here. On the night of your incident in Africa, it was morning here. I was preparing to go play a game of golf. As I was putting my golf bag in the car, I felt the Lord leading me to pray for you. In fact, the urging of the Lord was so strong, I called the men in this church together to meet with me here in the sanctuary and pray for you. Would all of those men who met with me on that day please stand up?"

The men who had met together to pray that day stood. When all were counted, the number was twenty-six!

Grow in Crosscultural Awareness

We've noted that God chose, in his work as Creator, to bless the earth with diverse peoples. The cultural mosaic of customs, colors, sounds, sights and traditions is God's gift to us. Unfortunately, we are often taught to fear what is different to us. This orientation is not biblical. Nor is it intelligent. We become enriched through our encounter with the spectrum of God's handi-work—and we become equipped to live effectively and meaningfully in the modern world. If we choose to take on the global mission of Christ as our life mission, then we will need to think through specific ways to grow in our crosscultural awareness.

First, we need to understand our own culture. Christians are often guilty of withdrawing from society under the misguided notion of "separating ourselves" from the world. In the effort to be true to Jesus' statement that we are "not of the world" (Jn 17:16), we practically leave the world. We lose our impact as light and salt. Societies express their pain and aspirations through drama, poetry, art, novels and music, to name a few of the standard forms. Christians should listen to the messages these forms convey (while exercising discernment). Through these mediums we draw a more accurate picture of our world and thus a more accurate picture of how we may respond.

This same skill, then, needs to be applied to other cultures. Christians who want to have a part in the global love affair with Jesus can simply identify a local group of people whose culture is quite different from their own. A white suburban person, for example, could make an effort to understand the urban African American. There is no shortage of music, art, films, books and events that can help one draw closer to this culture. Some white Christians who have launched out on this effort have been surprised to discover how much prejudice they carried toward people in their own country.

Next, identify people in your area who are transplants from another country. Look for ways to build relationships that will lead to an understanding of their culture. You'll discover that others just "think differently" than you do. What perhaps seemed to you as the "right way" or "reasonable way" to approach a situation can actually be seen as the foolish way in another culture. You may also discover different emphases: one society is strongly work-oriented, another community-oriented. The one gets projects done; the other builds friendships. The one shows up to meetings "on time"; the other never does. All of us have prejudices to overcome as we brush against other cultures—and it requires a good amount of grace, patience and humility to learn and grow.

Several years ago, a young Buddhist high-school student arrived in the United States from Thailand on an exchange program. He was placed with a Christian family, a fact that displeased him greatly at first. As time went on, things warmed up and Kriengsak became intrigued by the beliefs—and even more so the behavior and attitudes—of the Christian family. Over the months he had the chance to experience the love of Christ lived out there, to attend church with his host family and to meet their friends and acquaintances. He saw them resolve differences and ask forgiveness of one another. He was struck by stories he heard from the Bible and thought a lot about their implications.

Before long, Kriengsak asked how you become a Christian. And then, some time later, he made a commitment to Christ.

Kriengsak was an outstanding student. He accelerated throughout his college education and graduated with degrees through the Ph.D. in economics. Then he returned to Thailand, where he was immediately given a teaching position at the University of Bangkok.

Kriengsak returned to his country with a longing to share his faith with others. He started a church, called the Hope of Bangkok. In the next four years, that church grew very rapidly, to be the largest church ever in the history of the country. They established a Bible institute, a seminary and numerous satellite churches. They formed a mission called the Hope of Thailand, with the objective of forming a church in every community in their country. This all began through a host family in the United States inviting Kriengsak to live with them and share their life. What an incredible potential that represents for the kingdom! At the moment, there are 75,000 students from the People's Republic of China studying here in the United States—and perhaps 500,000 international students in all.

On one of my trips out of Madison, Wisconsin (Dan speaking), I was seated next to a gentleman from West Africa. He had been in Madison saying goodby to his African friends; he was on his way home after three years in the United States.

In the next three hours we had a long conversation about one another's lives, family, religion, faith and dreams. I learned that in his three years in the U.S., ours was the first conversation this man had with a Christian. And in three years, he had never been in an American home.

When we were parting, he kept saying to me, "Oh, how I have enjoyed this conversation! Oh, how I wish we were going to the same location! Oh, how I would like to discuss further the issues of faith. Oh, I wish we had met at the beginning of my time in America. Oh, how I wish that we would be living in the same place!" I shared his desires. What a tragedy, that thousands of international students come and go in this country without significant relationships with Christians. This gentleman went back to be the minister of agriculture for his entire country.

A couple was praying in their apartment in New York City. God caused one of them to pray for "the loneliest person in all of New York City." Since the U.S. had recently bombed Libya, they prayed for the Libyan ambassador to the United Nations. Getting up from their knees, they decided to invite the ambassador to their home for the Thanksgiving weekend. Lo and behold, he agreed to come.

They were a little nervous about this since they hadn't entertained internationals before. Yet they had a wonderful time together. Partway into the weekend, the ambassador ventured, "Could I ask you a question? Why did you invite me?" To which they answered, "We were praying for the loneliest person in Manhattan and you came to mind, and then we decided to invite you." Nothing more was said about this subject through the weekend, and they parted with great warmth.

They received a letter of thanks from the ambassador. Then, to their astonishment, they received a letter from Muammar Khadafy thanking them for their kindness to his ambassador! Also in the letter was an invitation for an all-expenses-paid trip to Libya as guests of the president. They went on the trip. They were royally received and given an audience with President Khadafy.

The president asked them why they had invited the ambassador, and they told him. Toward the end of the visit with the president, the American man asked if he could pray for him. Mr. Khadafy said, "Of course!" The American prayed for the salvation of Mr. Khadafy and his nation. When they finished praying, the president, with tears in his eyes, thanked the American and said that this was only the second time, to his knowledge, that he had been prayed for. He asked if the American would do this again. To this the American replied, "Of course I will, Mr. President. I'll pray for you every day." The President said, "Oh no. What I mean is, will you do this again on national television?" The American then had the opportunity to pray for Mr. Khadafy in front of television cameras that broadcast that prayer throughout the nation of Libya. He prayed for Mr. Khadafy's salvation and the salvation of his country.

What tremendous opportunities come when we listen to that still small voice of the Holy Spirit, nudging us in our prayers to be concerned about the lonely, the needy, the lost in our world.

Consider international travel as another means to grow in cultural understanding. If you are a student, you have myriad opportunities to study abroad. These options apply to any major or academic emphasis. If your commitment to the globe is serious, there is no reason why you couldn't plan two or three semesters abroad. And if you are attached to a Christian campus organization, then you are probably linked to several good options for summer mission projects in other cultures. Stepping into another culture is literally stepping into another world. And there is no way to understand that world except to go there. Afterward, world news, events and people will play a completely new role in your understanding of how the world hangs together.

Global Awareness

The term "World Christian," popular in the eighties, would be valuable to the members of today's Generation X. It should make a comeback. Behind this label is the idea that our Christianity is not limited to our own reference group or clique. We think in broader terms. We understand that what goes on in the world and in society at large is important to us as Christians. We don't want to live in isolation, and we want to be sure that our views of right and wrong have a large, planet-wide perspective, not a small, provincial one. God is a global God and therefore we are global people. In fact, built into this understanding is the notion that we cannot be effective contemporary Christians if we live isolated from the global pulse.

If we were doing our job right, the world would be following our lead in how to truly live as a global citizen. Unfortunately, too often it works the other way around. Being a World Christian means understanding how the wars and conflicts in the Middle East affect the gospel's work with Muslims; it means understanding how racism in America diminishes our ability to speak with ethical force in other parts of the world; it means seeing that our own inability to deal with the history of our treatment of Native Americans renders us powerless to understand the explosive force of nationalism in the world today—especially in the former Soviet Union and Eastern Europe. It means having a heart for the world's individuals, people groups and nations.

Vocation

As we reflect upon the diversity and immensity of this world's needs, we quickly realize that there is no place of insignificant service for Christians. Every deed of bringing tenderness to a broken world is a dignified work of love. Christians who would rate one form of service over another do not understand the nature of the body of Christ nor the nature of true ministry.

We become partners with God in feeling the pain around us, but we do not accept the unique role of God in presuming the "pain stops with me." That burden belongs to God. We can, however, look to God for our calling, for a specific role in alleviating some of the pain, for a vocation that is attached to global need and opportunity for kingdom work. God sovereignly guides Christians into these forms of service. And he does it individually. There is no set way to hear God or how to find that specific role.

Our calling is worked out in the context of serving right where we are. We don't wait for some light to guide us to our place of ministry—all the while sitting back because that magic moment has not come. No, we go to work with what we already know. And we do this in relationship with the body of Christ, the Christian family, the community of faith. We care for our roommates, family, friends, neighborhood acquaintances. We practice hospitality, visit the sick and prisoners, care for orphans, give generously of our time and money, pray long and hard for people in need and study the Word as though we were going to starve without it. And we listen carefully for the quiet voice of Jesus, we tune ourselves to be sensitive to the nudges of the Holy Spirit. Then, as we look back over time, we can chart the course where God has taken us. We never get to chart it in advance.

Most of us, at some point, receive a sense of vocation—a specific role of service. Some of us seem to get that insight in our first year of college and "lock in" immediately into the pastorate or medicine or whatever. Others of us find that vocational calling over a much longer stretch, sometimes not until a couple decades out of college. Not that God wasn't working through us prior to that vocational insight—much of our impact on society may happen outside the context of a job.

Questions we can ask along the way include: How do I see God working through me in this particular vocation? What kind of training should I receive? Where do I expect to serve God with this skill? What specific need do I expect to address with this training? It makes sense to try to link these insights to our actual training plans.

It also makes sense to acquire some of your training abroad—in academic exchange programs, internships or summer service trips. Employers are impressed by an academic résumé that shows a strong and certain orientation to the global context. You are less of a risk to them if your path shows clear thinking and determination along the way. If you plan to work in societies where the borders are closed to missionary visas, make sure that you graduate from a secular institution. This minimizes unnecessary suspicion regarding your reasons for entering another society.

Large numbers of today's generation are not going to end up with a "one-track" career. Experts are telling us now that members of Generation X will fill as many as seven different career descriptions in their lifetime. This should not be a deterrent to global service. Rather, it allows you to experiment with diversity. The opportunity is there to test the waters of the world and build up a rich set of experiences that contribute toward global service.

There are wonderful tales of college graduates who have spent a couple years in a refugee camp, then another on an environmental project and yet another in a discipleship role with church planters before settling into a longer vocational path. God is not limited by traditional employment boundaries, and so we should feel free to employ all our creativity on our journey to the wild. Most people eventually end up with a sense of "home," a sense that "I have found my place of calling for the next decade and, unless God shows otherwise, I'll devote myself to that course."

The Church

God is not employing Lone Rangers in the global mission. He is calling people who have a profound understanding that they are members of the family, the community of faith. Our witness to the world is essentially a family affair. People see how our love for God is expressed in our love for each other. And our very ability to become a living demonstration of the gospel depends on the combination of gifts God gives to the church—teaching, administrating, serving, caring and so on. And so it follows that to be a serious member of God's global call is to be a serious member of the church.

Now this will clearly take a different shape for each of us. Churches are very diverse in their expression of devotion to God. Some are highly liturgical, others very informal. Some primarily serve the family, others the outcast or oppressed. We need to work hard to find a church that will become our home fellowship.

The churches some of us know seem too traditional for us; they criticize or condemn our more contemporary ways of doing things. This just means our job is a little more difficult. At church we both give and receive. We need to find ways to learn from people who are entirely different from ourselves. These are good skills to have when we move into a crosscultural context. We also need to contribute our unique understanding of how the gospel is lived out in contemporary society. If we shy away from this demand in a local context where people disagree with our perspective, we will be less able to interpret the gospel's role in another society.

Some of us have been hurt by the church. Perhaps that has come in the form of racism, sexism, authoritarianism, sexual or emotional abuse. Unfortunately, the church is not free of these sins, and there are some Christians who will never return to the church because of the pain they have experienced at its hands. Part of life's maturation process is learning to incorporate our painful experiences into our sense of self. We want to eventually reach the stage where we are able to live healthy, compassionate lives despite—or maybe even because of—certain painful detours. We cannot rush the healing process in our lives, but if over time our pain prevents us from a vigorous life of service, we may have allowed the pain to become our god—and ourselves to become pitiful people. As we venture into relationship with other Christians, we become a living testimony of the power of the gospel when it goes to work in community. And that is something society desperately needs to see and hear.

There is one other angle where we always need to grow in our church life: The body is much larger than we think. If we are Baptists, for example, we may be suspicious of Presbyterians, and vice versa. That orientation is both unbiblical and destructive. If we cannot find unity and fellowship in the diverse body of Christ at home, we will never be able to do it abroad.

Linkage

At some point you need to begin thinking through the means by which God will be sending you into crosscultural ministry. In addition to the many Christian workers and "home missionaries" working within North America, more than 40,000 North American evangelicals are working full-time with a mission agency outside the boundaries of Canada and the U.S. These are organizations whose express purpose is to help Christians serve full-time in a crosscultural role. Many of these agencies are denominational structures and offer just about any form of vocational service. The majority, however, are independent groups focused on a specific form of outreach. There are more than 700 such organizations. God has a place for each of us.

Most of these organizations require their members to "raise support." This is a faith-filled process of going to churches and friends, requesting that they provide all the funds necessary for salary and ministry expenses. These agencies have a long track record of helping people raise their support.

Some of the denominational agencies, such as the Presbyterian Church—USA and the Christian & Missionary Alliance, provide a salary. And then there are groups such as Youth With A Mission (YWAM) which generally allow you to live month to month on whatever funds God provides.

Sometimes support-raising is a long process; sometimes the funds come in leaps and bounds, and seemingly out of nowhere. As people feel an urgent call from God to begin foreign service and mobilize their prayer circuit for the work they will be involved in, God shines through with his almighty faithfulness in miraculous ways.

One very recent happening took place in a small college in Iowa. From that one small InterVarsity chapter, four new graduates have joined the InterVarsity Link staff team. One has decided to head to Eastern Europe and three to the former USSR.

The three wanting to be placed in the former Soviet Union decided, being good friends, to work together in the support-raising process. They made joint presentations at the church they attended together while at college, as well as individually at their home churches in different states. From this one small community church, all three gained half of their support for a one-year term. One of these individuals received $9,000 in one month. That's his budget for the entire year! God truly does move in fund-raising situations.

Linking up with mission agencies can happen in several different ways. One is to attend mission conventions and talk with mission representatives in person. If you are a member of a denomination, inquire about its mission program. Ask about the process by which the church will help you move from pew warmer to crosscultural missionary. Vocational counselors at Christian colleges can also link you up with agencies that fit your sense of calling. We have listed a few resource organizations and publications at the end of the book. All of these will be valuable aids in getting you to where you believe God's Spirit has been nudging you.

You may be headed for a country where Christ's name is not very well known (for example, the Islamic, Hindu or Buddhist world). The most sensible and strategic way to enter these countries is to become a tentmaker (like the apostle Paul, who made tents to support his missionary work).

Today more than 400,000 North American Christians hold secular jobs abroad—many because they want to be a Christian presence there. You could choose to become a tentmaker. Your entry into the country of your choice will be legal and natural—people need your expertise. This is likely to be the key avenue for crosscultural ministry in the early twenty-first century, because many countries do not grant missionary visas. You may want to approach standard mission agencies to see if you can go as an associate with them. Even though you will not need to raise support and will not officially serve on their staff, several agencies have added "tentmaking" as a department and are ready to help you with training, international adjustment and legal issues.

You may want the professional help of an organization that exists to train and place Christians as tentmakers. If God has given you an entrepreneurial gift, consider beginning your own company to do business in a country where traditional missionaries are not permitted. Your business pursuits are legitimate, and you are your own employer, which offers you opportunity to adjust your schedule around relationships God is putting in your path. Your first line of witness is through the excellence of your work.

The Altar Call

"Whom will I send?" the Lord asks Generation X. "Who will go for me?"

That is both a generational question and an intensely personal one. And it has to be answered at both levels. It's an altar call. It really is that serious. We have attempted to put the call of the wild in front of you. Now it is yours;

it belongs to your heart. So we must ask: *What will you do with this call?* If not you who are Generation X, then who? If not now, then when?

Every generation stands at the burning bush, like Moses, and faces the option of saying yes to Yahweh. You don't have to say no—you can just do nothing, and that will be your answer. Detachment, apathy and selfish pursuit of comfort are all a clear response. But you have the opportunity of going against this cultural pull; the privilege of entering the most challenging, difficult, painful, rewarding and joyful station life offers; the option of pursuing the tug of the world, the call of God upon your heart.

Will this be what Generation X is remembered for? Will the world thank God for Generation X? We trust so. We believe that the hungry, homeless, lost, oppressed, orphaned and despairing citizens of today's world will bear testimony in heaven that the people who led the North American church into the twenty-first century did it with all the passion, grace and nobility that the cross deserves. There is no higher calling. There is no greater life to choose.

It's quite an adventure. Go for it!

Resources

We have listed a few publications that we think should be a part of anyone's starter kit to the world. They are worth the investment toward a future of compassionate living. And all of them combined cost less than a couple hundred bucks. It would be well worth budgeting for these as you explore what your future course may be.

Books
A series of five books constitutes "the complete activist guide to the world." Coauthored by Tony Campolo and Gordon Aeschliman and available from IVP, they are:

50 Ways You Can Be Prolife
50 Ways You Can Feed a Hungry World
50 Ways You Can Help Save the Planet
50 Ways You Can Reach the World
50 Ways You Can Share Your Faith

Christians have to struggle with their own brokenness as part of their journey to the world. God works with us—as we are—and is constantly changing us for the better as we strive to serve him. Dan Harrison tells his own story in a book that will help you deal with your brokenness while responding to God's call to the world:

Strongest in the Broken Places (IVP)

We also recommend a series of twelve Bible study books on global issues. Each has an introductory essay and six one-hour Bible studies. The Global Issues Bible Studies, also from IVP, are:

Basic Human Needs by Bryan Truman
Economic Justice by Jana Webb
Environmental Stewardship by Ruth Goring Stewart
Fundamentalistic Religion by Eva and Joshi Jayaprakash
Healing for Broken People by Dan Harrison
Leadership in the 21st Century by Gordon Aeschliman
Multi-Ethnicity by Isaac Canales
People and Technology by Mary Fisher
Sanctity of Life by E. Dawn Swaby-Ellis
Spiritual Conflict by Arthur F. Glasser
Urbanization by Glandion Carney
Voiceless People by Chuck Shelton

One other book will help you pray for the world. It is set up in 365 sections and takes you through every conceivable need in society. It is authored by Patrick Johnstone and available from Zondervan:

Operation World

Magazines

Three magazines will be of particular help. The first one is focused specifically on world missions and will be your ticket to all the issues surrounding this global pursuit. Six issues per year, $15.00.

World Christian
P.O. Box 3278
Ventura, CA 93006

Another magazine is devoted to the issues of global evangelism and social justice. It looks carefully at cultural issues and asks what it means to be a Christian in contemporary society. Ten issues per year, $25.00 (regular rate) or $15.00 (student rate).

PRISM
10 Lancaster Avenue
Wynnewood, PA 19096

Another publication is aimed specifically at Christians who want to be involved in Christian community development. It is a journal published by

World Vision International, a Christian humanitarian organization. Four issues per year, $25.00.

Together
919 W. Huntington Dr.
Monrovia, CA 91016

Handbooks

The *MARC Handbook* lists the 700 North American Protestant mission agencies with their activities, regions of service, addresses and statistics of personnel. $35.00.

MARC Handbook
919 W. Huntington Dr.
Monrovia, CA 91016

The *Short-Term Mission Handbook* is the comprehensive guide to involvement in short-term missions. $10.00.

Short-Term Mission Handbook
Berry Publishing
701 Main Street
Evanston, IL 60202

Organizations

Finally, here are a few resource organizations that can offer you information and assistance.

A group focused on the United States:
Christian Community Development Association
1581 Navarro Ave.
Pasadena, CA 91103

A group that publishes information on international Christian community development:
MARC
919 W. Huntington Drive
Pasadena, CA 91016

A group that will help you take initial steps toward the Unreached Peoples:

Caleb Project
10 West Dry Creek Circle
Littleton, CO 80120

A group that will help you take initial steps toward global environmental concerns:

Christian Environmental Association
P.O. Box 25
Colfax, WA 99111

A group that will help your church organize a special long-term program to become involved in missions: .

ACMC
P.O. Box ACMC
Wheaton, IL 60189

Two groups that will help you go into the mission field as a tentmaker:

Pacific Resources International
227 W. Trade St., Suite 2000
Charlotte, NC 28202

U.S. Association of Tentmakers (USAT)
P.O. Box 61163
Shawnee, OK 74801